2 -

GOLFFIRMATIONS

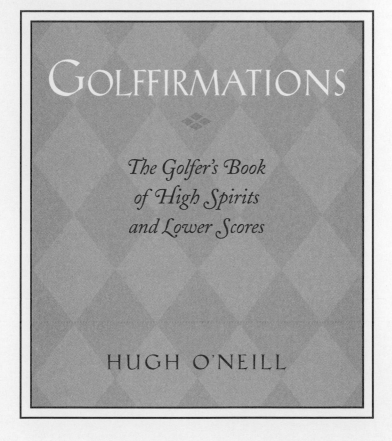

GOLFFIRMATIONS

The Golfer's Book
of High Spirits
and Lower Scores

HUGH O'NEILL

RUTLEDGE HILL PRESS® • *Nashville, Tennessee*
A Division of Thomas Nelson Inc.
www.ThomasNelson.com

Published by Rutledge Hill Press, a Thomas Nelson company,
P.O. Box 141000, Nashville, Tennessee 37214.

Library of Congress Cataloging-in-Publication Data

O'Neill, Hugh.
Golffirmations / by Hugh O'Neill.
p. cm.
ISBN 1-55853-928-X (hardcover)
1. Golf—Miscellanea. I. Title.
GV967 .056 2002
796.352—dc21
2001006003

Printed in the United States of America

01 02 03 04 05 — 5 4 3 2 1

To the men of Martindale

"We happy few, we band of brothers"

GOLFFIRMATIONS

INVOCATION

God Loves Golfers Most of All

 EVERY YEAR we spend billions of dollars and hours trying to shave a few strokes. We buy huge titanium drivers and magic can't-miss infomercial putters—for just five easy payments of $29.95! We read the instructional wisemen and take countless lessons. The well-heeled among us even make pilgrimages to study at the sacred sites—Orlando, Scottsdale, Hilton Head.

And yet, despite all the money and time and effort, we still send drives dribbling off the front of the teebox and boinging down the cart path into the greenskeeper's shed. We still nuke eight-foot putts into the water hazard guarding the green. Sad but true, for many of us, every time we address the ball, it's even money on a dead-pull into the Port-a-John.

How is it possible that after trying so hard, we're still so bad?

Simple.

We have knowledge but lack wisdom. Our spirits lack the serenity the game requires. We know what to do with our left arm and right heel, but we don't know how to feel about the game and, more important, about ourselves. Everything our brains know about a low takeaway or a high finish is trumped by all the human stuff—also known as doubt, impatience, inattention, and the caveman urge to just plain crush the ball. Our heads are educated, but our hearts are in the dark.

No more.

Here is a candle in that darkness. *Golffirmations* uses laughter and wisdom to break the bonds of mere knowledge and set free the good—okay, the *better*— golfer within. By helping you savor the joy, the simplicity, the honor at the heart of golf, it will probably lower your score. Even if it doesn't, it will make you laugh. And laughter isn't just good for your soul; it's also good for your blood pressure, respiratory function, and, hence, your life expectancy.

Each night before you play, cruise around in this book. Within, you'll find guidance for the challenges you'll face on the morrow. Some wisdom on tempo, on fellowship, on concentration, on enjoying each swing at the ball. Sleep on the sagacity of Bobby Jones, the Celtic vision of young Tom Morris, the torque of John Daly, and the joyful, harsh, full-throated humanity of the game. Let it enter your dreams, seep into your soul.

Carry *Golffirmations* in your bag and consult it mid round. When you see yourself coming undone, questioning whether a numbskull like you actually has a right to any of the world's oxygen, refresh yourself with Watson's underhanded wisdom. Read some post-duck-hook haiku to calm yourself after yet another yank into the left-hand woods. When a squirrel steals your ball, turn to a tranquility mantra to remind yourself of your devotion to the game that has shaped us all.

And, after your round, take up this book yet again. For there is consolation within—for that spike mark on 4 that ruined your entire round, that breeze that thwarted your backswing on 8, all those 5-irons foozled, and dreams deferred. *Golffirmations* uses laughter to light the path beyond pride and mere effort to the peace that passeth pars. It offers forgiveness for our frailty and hope for the next time out.

We are all of us seekers, enriched by our golfing journey, the mindful pursuit of who-knows-exactly-what—self-mastery, companionship, attentiveness, or perhaps the plain dappled beauty of trees, the soft enchantment of the wind, or the wide elations of the sky.

Take heart, my friends. God loves us, all golfers great and small. He wants us to keep swinging.

❖

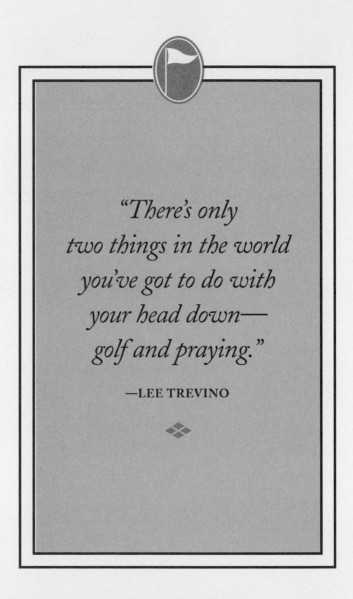

"There's only
two things in the world
you've got to do with
your head down—
golf and praying."

—LEE TREVINO

GOLFFIRMATION
1

On Keeping Faith Through a Four-Jack

O LORD, grant me the strength to forgive myself when I 4-putt from six feet away. Help me to remember that though I somehow turned a no-brainer birdie into a double bogey, life has some shred of meaning still, and the sun will rise tomorrow, warming the vast prairies of our great land, growing the amber waves. Help me to know that despite the acrid taste of self-loathing in my throat, though I want to break my putter in half and use the ragged shaft to perform radical angioplasty on my cowardly heart, somewhere flowers still bloom, children still laugh, and good-hearted women bake pies for the people they love.

❖

The Battle Hymn of the High Handicapper

 MINE EYES have seen the glory of some drive
    so straight and true,
    And I've endured a botched-up bunker shot
that stopped atop my shoe,
I have triumphed. I have staggered. I have foozled
    quite a few.
My handicap won't go down.

Glory, glory, I'm a 20.
Tales of woe, well I've got plenty.
But all that I remember is the pair of pars each round.
My handicap won't go down.

I've played for thirty years, and not a stroke have I
    improved,
I've taken lessons, read the Hogan, next to a golf
    course I have moved,
I have nightly dreams that somehow my swing I have
    at last grooved.
My handicap won't go down.

Glory, glory, I've got strokes.
Still that birdie on the last was not a hoax.
I striped a perfect drive, a sweet approach, and
    dropped a putt.
Can you say eagle, net?

I keep trying to get better, but I may be getting worse.
I'm no longer bright and cheerful, sometimes I even
    curse.
I've noticed that my partners on 18 are often terse.
My handicap's moving up.

Glory, glory, 21.
But all that I remember is the fun.
My follies fade completely, my few triumphs seem
    hard won.
My God, I love this game!!!

The Novel Known as Golf

NOVELIST E. M. FORSTER observed that the fundamental power of fiction derives from plain old plot, the reader's simple curiosity about what will happen next. Golf shares this glorious narrative engine. As we strut down the fairway headed to our tee ball—whether it's straight down the middle or plugged in Old Man's Marsh—we're in thrall to the possibilities.

What happens next? A crisply struck wedge, rising in graceful lob and settling, softly, snugly by the hole? Or a skulled line drive that caroms off a boulder and disappears into a drain pipe under the cart path? Or maybe a sixty-five-yard wormburner that zips down the fairway like a sharp single through the pitcher's box. Or maybe a whiff? Or maybe an eagle?

Who knows?

The possibilities call us forward.

As we climb up onto the green, the plot points put pepper in our pace. Will I sink this twenty-footer and savor the tweet of birdie? Or will I double-hit my lag and eventually sweat out a four-footer for a triple?

Golf is a novel. Will Huck help Jim escape? Will my 3-iron clear the water? Will Captain Ahab make peace with the whale? Will I ever escape this bunker? What happens next? That is the question.

Shakespeare's wisdom notwithstanding, that is the real question. What happens next? Its inquisitive allure explains our addiction to the game. We're hooked on the story, intrigued by the soap opera of the next shot, and the one after that, and . . .

We're hopelessly, happily trapped in the fascination of yet-to-come.

❖❖

GOLFFIRMATION
4

Some Words to Live By

WHEN BOBBY JONES was just starting out he found himself walking the fairway with the great Harry Vardon, clearly the pre-eminent player of his day. Jones played poorly but got some advice that took root and turned into a great career. "Don't give up. Just keep hitting it," said Vardon, six-time winner of the British Open. "Something good might come of it."

❖

GOLFFIRMATION
5

Of Time and the River of Golf

PULITZER PRIZE–WINNING novelist John Updike was once seated at a party next to a woman who remarked that life was too short for golf, an utterance that set the golf-addicted, but open-minded, 18-handicapper to thinking. Here's the scribe's considered conclusion:

"As soon say life is too short for sleep as say it is too short for golf. As with dreaming, we enter another realm, and emerge refreshed. Golf turns life inside-out; it rests the overused parts of ourselves, and tests some neglected aspects—the distance-gauging eye, the obscure rhythmic connection between feet and hands. For the hours and days it has taken from me, golf has given me back another self, my golfing self, who faithfully awaits for me on the first tee when I have put aside the personalities of breadwinner and lover, father and son. 'Golf lengthens life,' I should have told that young lady."

❖

GOLFFIRMATION
6

Of Heroes with High Handicaps

WHEN WE put the peg in the ground on the first tee, a journey begins. We leave home—the safe, congenial comforts of the clubhouse, the reassuring buoyance of the assistant pro as he sends you off—for the uncertainties of "out there." It matters not if it's our 407th loop around the home track or our first time around some sacred ground. Like pioneers who set out across the unknown, we're jumping off. Don't be deceived by the tameness of those khaki pants; we're heroes on a quest.

In no other sport do we traverse terrain, climb hills, descend into valleys, wade into water, trudge through deserts, and stumble through forests. In no other sport do we battle the wind, tear up the turf, and launch missiles into the air while calling on the virtues of patience, pluck, persistence, strength, delicacy, poise, serenity, wit, judgment, and faith. Enjoy the journey.

GOLFFIRMATION
7

Accentuate the Positive

UNDER NO circumstances carry a telescoping ball retriever in your bag. It reeks of blunder, marks you as a man prepared for failure. It sends bad vibrations throughout the bag, demoralizing all the other clubs. "Golfers who carry ball retrievers are gatherers, not hunters," wrote David Owen. "Their dreams are no longer of conquest, but only of salvage."

GOLFFIRMATION
8

Some Therapeutic Thou-Shalt-Nots

MOST OFTEN, the golfer is better served by focusing on positives. But not long ago, archaeologists found what appeared to be ancient golf scrolls of some sort in a small cave in Scotland. The wisdom is old and the prohibitions instructive.

THOU SHALT NOT:

. . . while walking up the 15th fairway, start a mental tally of your potential final total, if you but bogey in. Nor shall you imagine the glory of a personal best, thereby assuring you finish nine over on the last four holes.

. . . berate yourself in the middle of your swing, reliving the decision, now decades gone, to pass on the partnership with Bill Gates of Microsoft. You shall instead remember that God loves idiots most of all, and make a smooth thought-free pass at the ball.

. . . putt the ball into the lake.

Stay Behind the Ball

As YOU approach the teed-up, dimpled orb,
And settle into your stance,
Don't over-think the details, bro,
But one thought will boost the chance

Of a drive that flies out high and far
That makes your heart enthralled.
Just tell your body and your mind
To stay behind the ball.

Don't think of . . . well just, never mind.
Banish swing keys all.
Step up, go slow, and pal o' mine,
Just stay behind the ball.

Head back, weight, too; back shoulder low.
Note, it's a lovely day in fall,
But don't think anything else, kind sir.
Just stay behind the ball.

I'll end my poem if you agree,
To swing smooth and yeah, stand tall.
And what's that other tee-ball thought?
Oh, yeah, stay behind the ball.

GOLFFIRMATION
1o

The Answer to World Peace

SOME YEARS ago idealists tried to invent a universal language called *Esperanto*. The idea was that if everybody spoke the same language we could start moving away from war toward understanding. Good idea, except golf already is the universal language.

If you dropped a golfer from Brooklyn and a golfer from Kuala Lumpur onto a first tee in Saudi Arabia, there would be no misunderstandings. The players know the sequence of shots, the rules of absolutely everything, and, most of all, they understand what the other man is going through. Golf makes nonsense of language, of geography, of cultural clashes that are trivial compared to the ancient game. We don't need more treaties, just more tee times.

❖

Your Place in History

THE ORIGINS of golf present a puzzle to historians. Some argue that a Roman Empire ball-and-stick game called *paganica* was an early prototype. French chauvinists point to a game called *jeu de mail* as forerunner. The Dutch claim their ancient game, *kolven,* morphed into the U.S. Open. But though all of these games featured whacking some form of ball with some kind of club, none of them included a hole, the very essence—or is it the very absence—of the game? It took the Scots to come up with the hole.

Whenever you start down the first fairway, think for a moment about those fisherman on the east coast of Scotland, making their way back from their boats, and as they did idly whacking a stone with a handy stick toward a rabbit hole. It's a timeless legend. And you're part of the story—as are Mary Queen of Scots, the poet Wordsworth, Winston Churchill, Ike, and anyone who ever took a swing.

❖

All Golfers Are Brothers, Even the King

AT THOSE moments of high self-hate, when you've shot a million, it helps to know you're not alone, that when it comes to incompetence, failure, and heartbreak, golf gets us all—even the titans. We're all occasionally powerless before the severities of the ruthless game. So, before you melt down your clubs and turn your bag into an umbrella stand, consider this inspiring ineptitude by Arnie himself.

Los Angeles Open, 1961. Rancho Park Golf Course. First round. Ninth hole, 508 yard, par-5.

Palmer hits a good drive and decides to go for the green in two. It was his last hole, so he was looking for a big finish, thinking eagle all the way. Remember, this was in the days when 508 yards in two shots was more than driver, 6-iron. He takes a mighty Arnie whack with his 3-wood and blocks it right, out of bounds, onto the practice range. He drops a ball and proceeds to hit this one out of bounds—left this time.

Then, as though in instant replay, another ball o.b. right followed by another ball o.b. left. On his fifth try from that spot on the fairway, the King pastes one onto the deck. Two putts later, he writes down a 12.

Later, when asked how a player of his caliber could take a 12, he replied with characteristic style. "Simple," he said, "I missed a twenty-foot putt for an 11."

Most of us at least get to struggle and self-destruct in anonymity. Not Arnie. His ignominy was not on television. But the people at Rancho Park have made sure that it will be remembered. In an attempt to offer solace to high-handicappers, they commemorated Palmer's dozen by installing a bronze plaque at the 9th tee.

"On Friday, Jan. 6, 1961," it reads, "the first day of the thirty-fifth Los Angeles Open, Arnold Palmer, voted Golfer of the Year and Pro Athlete of the Year, took a 12 on this hole."

Feel better?

❖

GOLFFIRMATION
13

The Dawn Patrol

THE WHITE glare of the rising sun, pouring past the tree trunks. Dew glistening on blades and golfers, crusty-eyed, drowsy, and serene, sleep wrinkles on their faces. The boys, barely out of bed, set forth to do battle—half-awake, but summoned by the game. Drink in the *maybe* of each morning.

❖

GOLFFIRMATION
14

Of Tom Kite and Doing It Right

Tom Kite and Grant Waite were paired together in the third round. Waite's ball landed in ground-under-repair. He took a drop and then set up to the ball with one foot on the repair chalk line. Had he hit the ball he might have incurred a two- shot penalty for standing on the line.

Kite, who at the time had a one-shot lead on Waite, noticed his foot and said, "We don't need any penalties, that's for sure. At least, I don't." Waite re-dropped, took a proper stance and the next day, won the tournament by one shot over Kite.

When reporters tried to give Kite credit for his sportsmanship, he waved the kudos away in proper golfer style. "It would have been pretty chicken of me," he said, "to see him break a rule and then say, 'By the way, Grant, add two strokes.' That's not golf. That's those other sports where they're trying to get away with everything."

GOLFFIRMATION
15

Encouraging Words of Baby Birds

SAM SNEAD was the sultan of smooth. Everybody who ever saw him swing was struck by the silky tempo, the easeful grace, the rocking-chair cadence of his back-and-through. You can't swing like a whisper if your hands are squeezing too tight. Snead came up with a useful country boy metaphor to describe the neither/nor nature of the right way to take ahold of the club:

> Grip pressure is very important. You can't strangle the club with a hog killer's grip. You've got to hold it as if it were a little bird—gently but firmly. You don't want it to fly away, but you don't want to suffocate the poor thing, either.

The First Big Ball

THERE IS a hard-to-capture exhilaration at the moment our tee-ball rises up handsomely into the sky, a gentle draw bending it back toward the sprinkler heads. "In the golf education of every man," wrote P. G. Wodehouse, "there is a definite point at which he may be said to have crossed the dividing line—the Rubicon, as it were—that separates the golfer from the nongolfer. This moment comes immediately after his first good drive."

❖

GOLFFIRMATION
17

Remember: One Shot Can Fix It All

SURE, YOU dubbed it off the tee,
But say *Amen*, and just let it be.
Okay, your second was a sorry push,
That settled behind a bayberry bush.
But do not grouse or curse or hiss,
Take a breath, find your bliss.

Your third you strike like a woodchopper,
A squirrelly, ugly 13-hopper.
It stops in shame, perched on a mound,
A sidehill chip to the putting ground.
You stand despondent, full of rue,
Three stupid blows bid par adieu.

But here's the wonder/heck of our game,
Some magic's coming, as you take aim.
You crisp the chip, hit through it keenly,
It lands true soft, no, it lands serenely.
And tracks across the green with promise.
As smooth as, say, Fernando Lamas.

_____

Then drops into the cup with *Plock!*
Redemption for preceding schlock.
The lesson? Simple. Keep on striving,
The past is dead; the future, arriving.
Don't get sour, aspire to jolly,
Each coming blow can erase past folly.

It never happened, that foozled first,
Nor feckless 4-iron, nor wedge still worse.
The only truth is that Watson chip
That rolled so pure and found the lip,
Plunged into darkness for par, y'all,
Remember: one shot can fix it all.

So, stay in the hole, my boy, don't quit.
Eschew a funk, don't spit the bit.
Back slow, stay down, hit through the ball,
Remember: one shot can fix it all.

❖

Stand Tall, Like Tiger

WHEN TIGER WOODS arrived on the scene in professional golf, the superlatives started flying. In 2000, he won three major championships—two of them by historic margins. When he won the Masters in the spring of 2001, he became the first golfer to hold all four major titles at once. Analysts raved about his technique, the enormous power he generated, and about his great mental discipline and competitiveness. But the real lesson of young Woods, the truth that can be used by every high-handicapper, is an attitude that turns into a tip, a mind-set that shows itself in part of your swing.

Woods' finish has been hailed by the technicians. He hits through the ball with tremendous force around a firm left side. Of course, he stays down on the ball through contact. But then, as he surges toward the target, he starts to stand up straight, moving strongly toward his full erect height. Once he's watching the flight of the ball, he has risen to ramrod straight, his chest high. His finish oozes pride. Standing upright, he has the wholesome pride of a man well-pleased by his effort. If you ever feel as though your finish isn't strong, think about Tiger's prideful position. Don't be a meek little boy, ashamed that you've hit something hard. Stand tall like young Woods.

❖

GOLFFIRMATION
19

Of Game Hens and Small Dogs

IT IS possible that no single human movement has been described with more metaphors and similes than the golf swing. Countless teachers have come up with mental images involving buckets and church bells and Japanese fans; phone booths and train tracks and all manner of marriages between mind and matter. Here's a beauty of a don't-do-this sequence from the early days, courtesy of Horace Hutchinson, one of the pioneers in golf instruction:

> Let your arms be free from the body, and bent at an easy natural angle—not tucked in to the sides in the fashion of a trussed fowl, nor stuck out square like the forelegs of a dachshund, nor, again, stiff and straight in front of you like the arms of a man meditating a dive into water.

Got it?

GOLFFIRMATION
20

Why We Play

 CAN THERE be a better description of a golf shot struck just so than Ben Hogan's? "It goes from the ball, up the club shaft, right to your heart."

❖

GOLFFIRMATION
21

A Lesson from a Legend

MOST TEACHERS advise against imitation when it comes to the swing itself. But if you're having trouble staying behind the ball at impact, then at setup, try this signature head-tilt of the Golden Bear. By the way, Bobby Jones used it, too.

When Nicklaus (as in twenty majors) is about to swing, he turns his head the slightest bit backward, and looks at the back side of the ball with his front eye. This focus trick should help you keep your body behind the ball, where it can actually power your shot.

❖

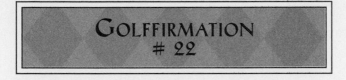

To a Butterfly, Lest She Be Disturbed

LORD, LET me swing gently with rhythm and tempo and grace. Let me imagine that there is a butterfly sitting atop my Titleist, and I am loathe to trouble her at her mild insect pursuits. Rather inform my swing with surgical calm, enabling me to deftly displace the ball from under her little insect pseudopods (feet) and deposit her safely, even tenderly, back on the dewy *poa annua*.

GOLFFIRMATION
23

The Beautiful Blankness

HEARTY, HAIL-FELLOW pleasantries to pro
Greens fees paid. Ball marker and tees
Claimed from counter jars.
Then the nubby pencil and . . . the card.
The record of what's to come, pregnant in its
    emptiness
The cleanest slate of human devising.
The small squares crying out for fewer.
Folded, slipped into haunch pocket,
Goes the small, crisp, creased cardboard of hope.

❖

Of Bad Breaks and Deep Lakes

AT THE 1980 Inverrary Classic, as Curtis Strange and his caddie were crossing a bridge to the 18th tee, the caddie was jostled by a spectator. He lost his balance, tipped forward, and the clubs in Strange's bag started to slide out and into the lake. When he managed to right himself, all that was left was 2-iron, 3-iron, 5-iron, and putter. The result: 2-iron tee-ball, 5-iron approach, and two putts for par.

The great golfers manage with what they've got. Promise yourself you will, too.

The Inspiring Range of the Great Game

OF ALL the writers who have tried to describe the heroic contradictions of golf, few have been more successful than Arnold Haultain, a little-known Canadian, who in 1908 penned a love letter to the greensward, a book called *The Mystery of Golf.* He managed to capture, in delightful oxymoron, the exotic mixture of delicacy and power required to master the game.

"In golf, you get the whole gamut of the muscular sense," Haultain wrote, "from the gigantic swipe at the tee to the gentle tap on the green." Our habit requires the A-to-Z of human skills, the talents of the stevedore and the surgeon. As Haultain put it, "Golf is a sort of Gargantuan jugglery, a prodigious prestidigitation, a Titanic thimble-rigging, a mighty legerdemain."

❖

GOLFFIRMATION
26

The Sound of Par

WE GENERALLY don't think of golf as a game of sounds, but here's a tip for making sure your three-footers all find the bottom. Stay down after sweeping away the putt. And don't peek at its journey. Just listen for the exquisite sound of balata hitting the plastic liner of the hole. Lifting your head is the greatest reason those short ones break our hearts. Relish the singular sound of success.

❖

GOLFFIRMATION
27

Embracing the Void

FOR OUR critics who claim golf is a mindless game, we have only something called condescending sympathy. They don't understand. But there is one golf moment in which it helps to get dumb, to turn off your mind. "When a putter is waiting his turn to hole out a putt of one or two feet in length, on which the match hangs at the last hole," wrote Sir Walter Simpson, one of the early chroniclers of the game, "it is of vital importance that he think of nothing. At this supreme moment he ought to fill his mind with vacancy."

❖

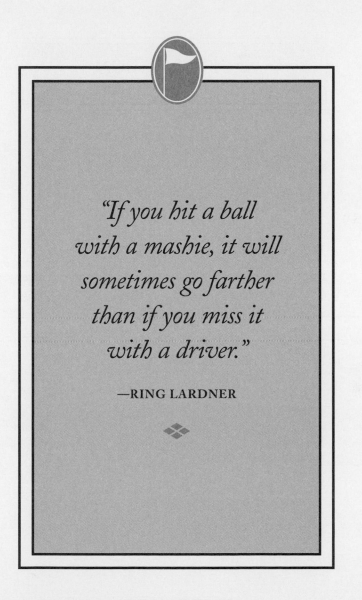

*"If you hit a ball
with a mashie, it will
sometimes go farther
than if you miss it
with a driver."*

—RING LARDNER

Two Days in July

MANY EXPERTS cite the 1977 British Open at Turnberry as the greatest head-to-head competition ever for the major championship. Jack Nicklaus and Tom Watson, paired together for the last two rounds, went at it, aging titan versus titan on the come. Time after time over two days, Nicklaus would open a lead—on one occasion as large as three shots—and Watson would each time come fighting back. Parry, thrust, jab, counter-punch—choose your combative metaphor—they fired matching 65s in the third round. And in the final round, when they came to the 17th tee, they were dead even. Watson lasered his 3-iron second onto the dance floor of the par 5 and two-putted for birdie; Nicklaus missed the green in two, chipped up to within three-feet, and then missed the short putt for birdie. It was the first time Watson had the lead during their mano-a-mano match.

Then on the par-4 18th , Watson put his approach two feet from the pin. Nicklaus was way right in heavy rough, his swing partially blocked by a gorse bush. A lesser competitor would have known he couldn't win. He not only needed to get up and down from an impossible spot, he needed Watson to miss a two-footer. Nicklaus somehow muscled an impossible 8-iron onto the deck, thirty-five feet from the hole. With Watson's ball just two feet from victory, Nicklaus studied the bending putt with extraordinary care, bent over it in that characteristic question-mark hunch and proceeded to drop the putt into the cup for birdie. All of this, mind you, after missing a mere three-footer on 17.

Watson made his putt and won the day. But Nicklaus teaches the lesson. Stay in the hole. Discipline. Work. Attention. Never quit. The secret is to care about everything.

❖

You're Better than This Pro

A PRO named Jerry Pate had a fifty-foot putt for eagle in the 1982 World Series of Golf. He missed it, then missed the comebacker for birdie, and the short putt for par. Disgusted, he jabbed at the bogey tap-in, missed that, too, and worse yet, hit himself in the foot with the ball. Two-stroke penalty. He eventually wrote down 9, having turned a potential eagle into a quad. Feel better, don't you?

❖

GOLFFIRMATION
30

A Whole New World

THE FIRST tee makes life new. There is no explaining the hopefulness that a golfer brings to that sacred spot. Somehow, a man who is a complete dub, who struggles in the land north of 100, arrives just sure, just dead-solid sure, that this time he's found it. With the first fairway stretching out in front of him, he will swing with serenity and strength; he will not hit the ball but allow it to get in the way of his swing. He's sure his history is not prelude. This time the golfer within will emerge.

In no other arena of life is such cockeyed dreaming, such hopefulness, routine. True, it lasts for an instant only, but those few steps up to the teed ball must be cherished.

❖

The Master on the 18th Green

BOBBY JONES is considered by many the finest golfer of all time. Whether he was the best or only top five is of no matter. There's no debate that the Daddy of the Masters was a remarkable man, a paragon of sportsmanship and honor, the very incarnation of golf spirit and golf grace. He was one of those precious people—someone to admire.

In 1950, when Jones was but forty-eight, he was diagnosed with rare degenerative disease of the spinal cord called syringomyelia. And over the next twenty-one years, the disease crippled him, inch by inch claiming the galvanizing athleticism with which he had won thirteen major championships between 1923 and 1930. His condition was complicated by heart trouble, and his body withered away. For the last part of his life, he was confined to a wheelchair and endured great pain with stoic style, refusing to dwell on his illness. Indeed, Jones would brook no talk of it during the many pilgrimages admirers made to his home.

A story is told of an old friend who, when visiting Jones in his cabin hard by the 10th tee at Augusta National, was clearly upset by the frailty of Jones' condition. Sensing the friend's ache, Jones reassured him with a gallant reference to the glorious discipline of the game. "Now, now, we won't have that," he said in both scold and consolation. "We have to play our ball as we find it."

❖

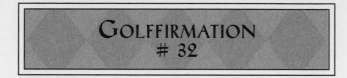

GOLFFIRMATION
32

To Rush Would Be a Crime

YOUR WHEELS are coming off. You've thinned two, fatted one, and skulled a baby wedge. Call to mind the simple tempo wisdom of Bobby Jones, the man who gave America the game: "Nobody ever swung a golf club too slowly."

❖

Let It Be

ONE OF the great amusements of golf is the desperation of our search for its secret. We look to physics, to meditations, to equipment, to elaborate pre-shot routines, to the disciplines of eastern mysticism. Perhaps no single piece of advice more fully captures the absurdity of our quest than the instructional imperative from *Caddyshack*, the greatest movie of all time. "There is a force in the universe that makes things happen," sayeth Ty Webb, the preppy lay-about golfer played by Chevy Chase. "All you have to do is get in touch with it, stop thinking, let things happen, and be the ball."

Of course, it's so simple. Just be the ball.

❖

The Legend of Crumpin-Fox

EVERY GOLFER knows the agony of the huge divot, the swing that turns the golf club from an instrument of surgical finesse into a gravedigger's shovel. Who among us hasn't buried the clubhead in the earth, become brother to the miner? Let us take a moment to humbly remember the greatest divot ever made.

The setting: the 16th fairway of The Crumpin-Fox Club in Bernardston, Massachusetts. The golfer: Let's call him Everyman. He swung, or rather chopped down, as though, it appeared, trying to cleave a log in twain. The club thwumped into the earth with a sickening thud, and sliced a giant pelt of sod out of the greensward. The divot must have been six inches wide and close to a foot long. It looked like a remnant at a carpet sale.

For a moment, Everyman and his comrades didn't know where the ball had gone. Until they realized it was under the divot, buried under the blanket of earth, which had rolled forward and smothered it. Now, that was a divot—weighing in at close to three pounds.

Remember the assignment: Clip the ball crisply off the turf (wedge shots excluded). To this day the beaver pelt, for such is the name of the legendary turf toupee, haunts the golf dreams of all the men who bore witness.

❖

The Demon of Distance

You KNOW that nuclear-powered driver you paid a small fortune for? Break it in half. Better yet, give it to the guy you play against most. Let delusions of distance wreck his game.

Who among us doesn't dream of powering the ball a country mile? We are a prodigious people, born in the land of Babe Ruth. We all want to be Long Man off the tee, the last to play his second. But for most of us, the driver—the club with unlimited potential to send the ball flying—is our enemy. When we heft it, the slugger gene takes over, the lizard part of our brain that aspires to the tape measure home run. We take a gorilla swing that sacrifices precision for power. Try a 3-wood and see if your swing isn't smoother and your tee-ball plenty long. The length of your drive is not an indicator of your worth as a person, or maybe even a golfer.

❖

GOLFFIRMATION
36

Some Inspiring Prohibitions

 THOU SHALT NOT:

. . . stand over the ball and re-play a mental videotape of every similar shot you've ever smashed into the greenskeeper's tool shed . . .

. . . pretend to be overtaken by a coughing fit in the middle of your opponent's backswing.

. . . ever, even if you drain a fifty-foot snake to beat your archenemy, shout the phrase, "I'm da man."

❖

GOLFFIRMATION
37

Of Greatness and Gut Shots

FOR A time during the late eighties, early
nineties, Greg Norman was clearly the best
golfer in the world. He won the British Open
in 1986 and 1993 with two of the great rounds ever
played. Tom Watson described Norman's third round
63 at Turnberry in '86 as the finest round by any player
in any tournament in which he had been a competitor.
Of Norman's closing 64 to win at Sandwich seven
years later, Bernhard Langer said virtually the same
thing. But Norman embodies the spirit of golf not for
his successes alone but for his unusual blend of triumph and heartbreak.

At least four times he's lost tournaments to golf
shots holed from bunkers or other impossible places.
Two of the tournaments were majors. In 1986, Bob
Tway holed out a bunker shot on the 72nd to steal the
PGA title. The next spring in a play-off at the Masters,
Larry Mize chipped in from an impossible spot to
beat Norman again. On top of his bad luck, Norman's

history includes one of the most celebrated collapses in professional golf history. He started the final round of the 1996 Masters with a six-shot lead over Nick Faldo. He shot a 78 and lost the tournament by five strokes when Faldo shot 67.

Through it all, the great victories, historic rounds, the lighting bolts that hit him, and the failures that were all his own, Norman has been the poster boy for sportsmanship. He understands the brutal joy of the game. "The failure is what makes succeeding so sweet," he said. "In golf, failure is a great thing, an absolutely necessary thing."

GOLFFIRMATION
38

There's No Place to Hide

LEGEND IS that back in the 1950s, comedian Jackie Gleason took Toots Shor, the celebrated saloon-owner and beginning golfer, out to play with him. Shor was so bad that when he asked Gleason what he should give the caddie, Jackie replied, "Your clubs."

❖

GOLFFIRMATION
39

Finding the Feel

THE GRAIL of golf is that vague thing known as a "feel" for the clubhead. The most holistic of the teachers believe that somehow bridging the gap between your grip and the clubhead is the single most important key to allowing a perfect swing—or rather, a good-enough swing—to unfold. Though it's easy to be confounded by the language, it's hard not to understand when you develop this pre-shot habit, recommended by Jim Flick:

> Hold your club straight up, perpendicular to the ground, and feel the weight of the clubhead. Can't feel the clubhead at all, right? Too light.
>
> Now hold it straight out in front of you, parallel to the ground. Causes a little pull at the top of your wrists and forearms, right? Too heavy.
>
> Now hold it pointing halfway between the first two positions. Close your eyes. Focus on the weight you feel. That's the weight you want to feel throughout your golf swing.

❖

GOLFFIRMATION
40

In Moments Dark, a Shining Fact

ARNOLD PALMER once summarized the addiction of golf by observing that despite the game's huge vexations, nobody ever gives it up. The King shall not be gainsaid here. But we all have the moment of temptation.

They usually come late in a star-crossed round, when we're squishing through yet another lateral hazard, wondering how in God's good name we can play this game for years and still be so astoundingly bad at it. In a painful flash of insight, we suddenly see a lost soul, a fool who has wasted thousands on lessons and equipment and greens fees, money that might have paid Stan Jr.'s way through Tulane or even been donated to help cure cancer.

When your moment comes, when you're tempted to lose faith, fight despair with a single powerful truth about the game.

Golf has been played on the moon.

In 1971, astronaut Alan Shephard hit a 6-iron from a bad lie in the Sea of Tranquility.

No other game has been played on the moon—not football, not chess, not soccer, not hoops, not marbles, not polo, not hockey, not bridge. Golf alone has triumphed over space and five-sixths of gravity.

Golf has been played on the moon.

An accident? Not hardly.

Golf is divine, touched by our celestial ambitions. It embodies the habit of hope that makes us human. Golf may appear to be no more than a bunch of pasteled popinjays whacking a ball for no apparent reason. But golf is much more than it appears. We have a duty to play it, to reach, to aspire. Remember . . .

Golf has been played on the moon.

P.S. After Shephard returned to earth he got a note from the Royal and Ancient Golf Club in Scotland, chiding him for not repairing his divot.

Hey, rules are rules.

❖

GOLFFIRMATION
41

On Remembering Swing Keys

O LORD, please grant my brain the wisdom to remember 13 different swing keys every time I address the ball. Especially help me (1) to swing as though trapped in a barrelful of honey; (2) to turn my shoulders as though I'm trying to slip sideways through a closing subway door on the Times Square shuttle—while carrying a standing lamp; (3) to squeeze the club with the last two fingers of my left hand as though I were milking a cow and couldn't, for some reason, use my other fingers.

Most important of all, teach me the mindfulness to be sure that every time I address the ball, an imaginary line drawn through my right ear and my left heel always points—during the summer, in the Northern hemisphere—directly at the last star in the handle of the Big Dipper.

GOLFFIRMATION
42

Make Your Home on the Range

THE GREAT Ben Hogan was a fiend for practice. He spent countless hours drilling, hitting shot after shot with care, attending to every detail of swing and ball flight. To Hogan it was all about diligence and effort and hard work. The secret of golf? Nothing fancy or clever, not for the Hawk. "It's in the dirt," he said. "You've got to dig it out."

Bring some buckets, boys.

❖

Don't Think About the Water, Fred

DON'T THINK about the water, Fred,
It's not in play, think dry.
  Just true a 6-iron to the deck,
That pond's not there, big guy.

Don't think wet or splash or plunk
Of submarines or scuba.
Don't think bath or dunk or swim
Of Jamaica or Aruba.

Think dry, brave Freddie, terra firma.
Don't view the lake as ticklish.
Just see the ball a' safe on land,
And you'll come up dry like Nicklaus.

Breathe deep. Relax. Back low and slow,
Hit crisply through balata.
Finish the swing, turn hips to hole,
And you'll fly the looming wata.

The Uncanny Intelligence of Golf Clubs

IF NONE of your putts are dropping, you may need to change putters. Sometimes the look of a flat stick is at odds with your visual something-or-other. But as you shell out big bucks for a new blade, keep in mind the wisdom of Lee Buck Trevino: "Those new putters have a way of quickly figuring out who's holding them."

Why We Play

IT'S THE sweetest sound of all the many sounds in this world—the contact when an iron is trued from the fairway. That *whoosh*, at once whispery and yet somehow slightly fierce, like a vaporous arrow piercing time. The sound that golf's literary chronicler John Updike called "a pleasant tearing sound, as if pulling a zipper in space."

GOLFFIRMATION
46

You're Better than This Pro

TOMMY NAKAJIMA is one of the top Japanese golfers in history, but he too is our brother, another victim of the brutality of the game. It's 1978, and Nakajima is two shots off the lead in the second round of the Masters when he arrives at the 13th tee. Here's what happened:

His tee-ball catches a branch and drops into Rae's Creek that runs along the left side of the fairway. Takes a penalty drop, whacks his third out of the woods within wedge distance. Up and down for par, right? Nope. He shorts a wedge into the stream guarding the green—4. He tries to hit it out of the water—5. The ball moves only far enough to hit him in the foot—two-stroke penalty: 6 and 7. He tries to hand his muck-covered club for cleaning to his caddie. They drop it into the hazard—two-stroke penalty: 8 and 9. He wedges out into a bunker behind the green—10, blasts onto the deck—11, and two-putts for, that's right, 13.

It's enough to make a man proud of that snowman from yesterday's round.

❖

GOLFFIRMATION
47

The Wisdom in a Waggle

EVERY GOLFER knows the tension that can build up in your body just before you start your swing. If it locks you up, it's nearly impossible to make a smooth swing. Most experts suggest some movement to break the tension and kind of glide you into the backswing. If you feel tense before your takeaway, try using a slight forward press of the hands, and then rebound into the backswing.

The waggle, a small waving and hovering of the club, just before your swing, can loosen up the works.

❖

GOLFFIRMATION
48

The Cradle of the Game

THE OLD Course at St. Andrew's is arguably the most hallowed ground in golf. American after American, from Bobby Jones to Sam Snead, has started off skeptical of its barren terrain and ended up an enthusiast, devoted to its diabolical demands. To understand the course's charms, consider the tale of a St. Andrew's caddie who saw that his man's ball was at the base of a rise with no view of either the fairway or the green. He pointed skyward, calmly saying, "Just hit that cloud." The ball landed six feet from the cup.

Golf is played under the vault of heaven. Be humble and inspired by the stage.

❖

GOLFFIRMATION
49

Hope Springs

"GOLF, IT seems, must be learned afresh each time we tee off, and if on the one hand it humbles us with a sudden collapse of some aspect of play we thought we had mastered, it, on the other hand, always holds out, perhaps even more to the inept than to the expert, the hope of dramatic improvement."

– John Updike

❖

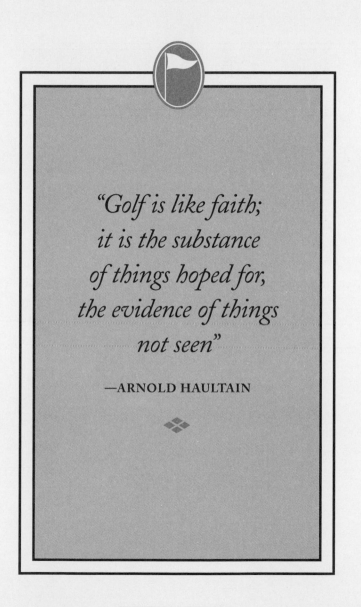

*"Golf is like faith;
it is the substance
of things hoped for,
the evidence of things
not seen"*

—ARNOLD HAULTAIN

GOLFFIRMATION
50

The Phantom of the Perfect

"WHAT LEADS you on in golf is this. You think a perfect pitch of excellence can be attained. . . . Always you can imagine a longer drive, a more accurate approach, a more certain putt; never, or rarely ever, do you effect all three at every hole in the course. But all men who are golfers always live in hopes of accomplishing them. . . . Hope springs eternal in the human breast, as progress, as development, is the one incontestable implanted in all things living, the cosmic principle, the law of heaven and earth, the motive of all effort, the germ of all action— the phantom of the perfect success flits over before the ardent golfer."

— *Arnold Haultain,* The Mystery of Golf

❖

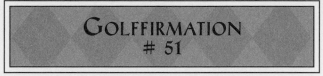

GOLFFIRMATION
51

The Daintiness of the Game

TEACHER BOB TOSKI got through the chaff to a useful kernel: "The club weighs less than a pound. The ball weighs less than two ounces. We don't need to prepare for violence."

❖

The Shape of Putts to Come

PAUL RUNYAN, a small guy who managed to win twenty-nine times on Tour, was, you guessed it, a master of the short game. He used chipping and putting to demolish Sam Snead in the 1938 PGA Championship, beating him 8 and 7 for the most one-sided finals victory in the match play history of the event. Runyan used a putting drill, which will help you to develop confidence and versatility around the hole and toughen your flat stick game.

Drop three balls a yard from the hole. Hit the first putt, so the ball just drips over the front edge on its last turn. Then, hit the second one so it rolls briskly into the cup. The last ball you're going to ram into the back of the hole, see if you can make it hop up before dropping in. The goal is to see the shape of each putt, to create a mental picture of how you're going to make the shot.

Runyan did the same drill with longer putts, too.

He'd try to make a twelve-footer by playing lots of break and dying it into the hole. Then he'd try to make the same putt, hitting it hard, taking out as much break as possible.

It's important to both see the ball going in and picture the shape of its journey.

❖

GOLFFIRMATION
53

Of Winds and Words

ALONE ON the fairway, the golfer is small, dwarfed by the vastness of sky, the rolling surges of earth. His physical weapons are humble, some small sticks carried in a quiver. But he's armed with one invisible mental tool as well: a thought. An empowering phrase about his left elbow or his right foot, some image of rotation or of pace. A phrase like "Shoelace end facing the target" can shrink the world and sometimes make the mind a master. The golfer's swing thought is a charm, a verbal amulet to keep him safe in a scary sea of space and air and sometimes wind and rain.

❖

GOLFFIRMATION
54

Golf is Truth, Truth Golf

WILLIAM WORDSWORTH played golf, but according to Sir Walter Simpson, the verse-maker was not well-suited to the game: "The poetic temperament is the worst for golf. It dreams of brilliant drives, iron shots laid dead, and long putts holed, while in real golf, success waits for him who takes care of the foozles and leaves the fine shots to take care of themselves."

❖

GOLFFIRMATION
55

Mending Mother Earth

You START to anticipate the pleasure halfway to the green. That 9-iron you just smoothed from 125 yards fell onto the green like a bean bag, hopping but a foot from where it struck. As you stride toward the deck, you picture the small impact crater, the dimple in the green that is testament to your surgical skill. You climb onto the green, take a quick glimpse at the line of the ten-foot putt remaining, and then with a small tool you turn to your duty of ball-mark repair. Proud of your damage and equally proud of your fix, you prep the dance floor so all putts will run true.

❖

Hey, He Helped Tiger

BUTCH HARMON, one of the great teachers, counts among his pupils the great Tiger Woods—the only man to have ever held all four major titles at the same time. Harmon's a big believer in the art of boldness. "Sometimes we get so afraid of hitting bad shots," he says, "we don't let ourselves hit good ones."

❖

GOLFFIRMATION
57

From Bad to Verse

THE ANTHOLOGY of our mistakes,
Can render golfers teary.
And the vocab of our blunders, boys,
Could make Noah Webster weary.

The skull, the shank, the double hit,
The grounder that's a rocket,
The foozle, sky ball, screaming hook,
Swings that tear shoulders from the socket.

The push, the pull, banana slice,
The fatted shot, the thinned
The too-hard putt, the stubb-ed chip
The ball off brother's shin.

The fluff, the skite, dear Lord, the whiff,
Our errors, they are myriad.
But set your mind to smooth and full,
And words can't hurt you. Period.

GOLFFIRMATION
58

Even Eeyore's Creator Knew

 GOLF OFFERS transcendent pleasures. No matter if we are reverse-pivoting, deep-divoting oafs, golf is joyful, relaxing, fulfilling, wholesome, mysterious, and somehow ultimately engaging. The man who wrote *Winnie the Pooh* captured its sweet democracy. "Golf," wrote A. A. Milne, "is the best game at which to be bad."

❖

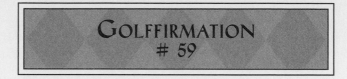

GOLFFIRMATION
59

Full Fathom Five the Trophy Lies

DURING THE PGA Las Vegas Invitational in 1991, Mark Brooks, who had won two tournaments that year, dropped his final tee-shot of the fourth round onto the green at the par-3 9th hole. He's planning a closing birdie when he marks his ball, and tosses it to his caddie. One problem: the caddie isn't looking, and the ball rolls into the lake guarding one side of the green.

The rulebook says that if you don't finish the hole with the same ball you hit off the tee, it's a 2-stroke penalty. So, Brooks takes off his shoes and socks, wades into the water, and starts searching, feeling with his hands and feet. At first, he's only in up to his shins. He finds a ball and tosses it up onto the bank. Not his. He finds another. Not his either. Gradually, he moves farther and farther out into the lake, groping with his toes, and bending over to toss ball after ball that is not his onto dry land. He found eighteen anonymous drowned golf balls before he gave up and emerged from the lake, covered in muck up to his shoulders. The crowd and even Brooks roared.

Moral: Never toss your ball in the direction of the drink. An error by your caddie could cost you the club championship.

❖

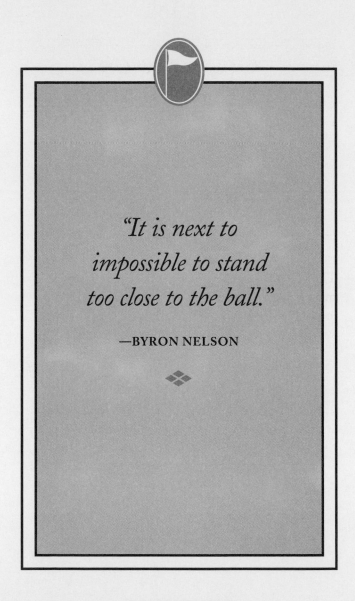

"It is next to impossible to stand too close to the ball."

—BYRON NELSON

GOLFFIRMATION
60

Of Care and Flair

NO TREASURE has ever been more elusive and keenly sought than what Walter Hagen called the "educated languor" of the golf swing. The golfer is a pilgrim in search of the impossible. He must be careful but never tense, precise, yet somehow loose. He needs to array all his body parts just so, and yet manage the methodical configuration without stiffness. Back in the nineteenth century, one of the first distinguished scribes of the game summarized the lifelong search succinctly. A golfer needs to cultivate "infinite carefulness," wrote Horace Hutchinson, before adding an impossible warning: "Do not be so scientific as to lose all dash."

Always remember, friends, a golf swing requires some dash.

❖

The Grace of an Ace

GOLF HAS a way of offering up grace notes, blessings from out of the blue. Gene Sarazen was the first man to win the career grand slam, the author of the single-most-famous shot in history, the inventor of the sand wedge, and by late in his life, a beloved senior statesman of the game. During his last British Open, the 1973 edition held at Troon, the seveny-one-year-old Squire made a hole-in-one at the famous postage stamp 8th hole. In golf, blessings abound.

❖

GOLFFIRMATION
62

A Sound, a Summons to Savor

As YOU lift your bag out of the trunk, the clubs clatter and click head to head—metallic, precise slaps as though rousing each other for the battle. Time to go, boys, the game's afoot. A techno-whisper, a reveille, akin to the clicking of a gun barrel in spin, an intimation of weaponry and will, a clarion of congenial clash to come. Hear the summons. Answer the call.

❖

GOLFFIRMATION
63

A Prayer for Putting Patience

O LORD, inspire my eyes. Let me somehow see the proper line for this forty-foot downhill snake. Let the path of this putt be illumined by the phosphorescence of thy love. Failing that, O Lord, grant me the courage to endure when I play the putt to break six feet left and it dives instantly right, skittering away from the hole and off the green, coming to rest against the trap rake for the bunker that guards the green.

❖

GOLFFIRMATION
64

The Golden Bear on Making Movies in Your Mind

"I NEVER hit a shot, even in practice, without having a very sharp, in-focus picture of it in my head. It's like a color movie. First, I see the ball where I want it to finish, nice and white and sitting up high on the bright green grass. Then the scene changes quickly and I see the ball going there: its path, trajectory and shape, even its behavior on landing. Then there's a sort of fade-out, and the next scene shows me making the kind of swing that will turn the previous image into reality. Only at the end of this short Hollywood spectacular do I select a club and step up to the ball."

— Jack Nicklaus

❖

GOLFFIRMATION
65

Of Precision and Pretense

JUDGING DISTANCE is one of the fundamental skills of golf. You've bisected the fairway with a huge drive. You're in position A. You're still 50 yards from the ball when you start trying to measure the length of your approach shot. You look for the bush that marks 150 yards. You look down for a sprinkler head with a yardage. Once you've got a reliable figure, then you start pacing, carefully stepping. You are an expert surveyor bringing precision to the task at hand.

Then starts the golfer's math: 157 to the middle, but the pin is up so -4. You bend, pluck some grass and toss it into the air. Slight breeze in your face, that's +3, maybe +5. On and on go the calculations. You're Wernher Von Braun, estimating arc, velocity, and throw weight for every conceivable variable.

Of course, all you know about your 7-iron is that it travels somewhere between 130 and 160 yards. And in any case, you have virtually no distance control. But none of this makes you less meticulous in your measurements, and that's how it should be. Who cares? Enjoy your calibrations, rocketeer. The charade is a sweet ceremony, a permissible pretense we share as brothers. Until you actually hit the ball, your secret is safe.

❖

GOLFFIRMATION
66

We Will Make the Best of Our Blunders

GOLF IS a game of managing your misses. Avoid disaster, take care of your ball. Remember Ben Hogan's remark that even when he was playing his best, in every round he only hit about five or six shots just the way he intended. Perfection is a dream. Keep the ball in play.

❖

GOLFFIRMATION
67

Hale, the Whiffing Hero

DURING THE third round of the 1983 British Open, held at Royal Birkdale, Hale Irwin, now three-time winner of the U.S. Open, whiffed on a two-inch putt. How? On the 14th hole, his birdie putt from twenty-five feet fell away at the last instant, and a disappointed Irwin walked up to the ball and tried to backhand it gently into the cup. But his putter hit the ground first and somehow bounced completely over the ball! Of course, golf being an exacting game, he finished the next day one stroke away from a play-off with Tom Watson, who took home his fifth claret jug.

You, my friend, would have made that two-incher.

❖

GOLFFIRMATION
68

Those Tempting Trees

I THINK that I shall never see,
A golfer who understands a tree.
"It's 90 percent air," they shout with hope.
But he who doesn't punch out is a dope.

Get back to the fairway, then slap a wedge close,
And putt for par after taking your dose.
You ask what this blessed game is about?
Hey pilgrim, don't panic. Punch it out.

That trees are airy is not germane,
Since the ball in flight has got no brain.
It's a Strata or Maxfli, not a smart missile,
And can't turn left 'mid oak or thistle.

And yet the golfer takes his stance,
Convinced somehow he has a chance
To hit right through God's great green geyser.
Bad plan, my friend. Here's the reason why, sir:

You'll hear a tick or thwock or thud,
When the ball hits foliage or wood,
And drops or caroms who knows where.
It can't find the 90 percent that's air.

So stay humble, and modest,
Don't damage the trees.
Punch it out . . . Punch it out . . .
I'm begging you, please.

❖

The Agony of This Close

WHEN OUR faith gets tested, we turn to trusted parables to sustain our spirits. A story is told of a golfer, a writer who was competing in the family golf tournament, the annual match with his seven brothers. He was fifty yards off the 18th green, needing to pitch the ball on and 2-putt to win what is perhaps the most cherished crown in golf.

What happened?

He shanked the chip, dead right, and skited the ball into the woods. From fifty yards away, dead center, he shanked a baby wedge. And then, from behind a giant mushroom, he struggled to get down in 4. He still has nightmares, though it happened five years ago and his life has had some joys since then. He takes comfort from a player who blew a less important tournament. When people ask Doug Sanders if he still thinks about a short putt he missed to lose the 1970 British Open, he says, "No, sometimes it doesn't cross my mind for a full five minutes."

❖

Three, Two, One . . . Contact

AMID THE thousand semi-technical pieces of advice, about arm angles and swing paths, it's easy to forget a central truth: "It doesn't matter if you look like a beast before or after the hit," sayeth the slashing Spaniard Seve Ballesteros, "as long as you look like a beauty at the moment of impact."

Ballesteros had another simple truth when asked the secret of golf. "To forget," he replied. Remember that.

GOLFFIRMATION # 71

We Will Enjoy the Fruits of Folly

 YOU EYE the twenty-two-foot bender, and line it up with a precision that would do a neurosurgeon proud. Four inches outside right. You stand over it with the serenity of a swami, draw back the blade, and then proceed to pull the putt well left with all the deftness of a great ape. You groan, despairing in your clumsiness, shriven that you've been playing the game twenty years and haven't mastered, well . . . anything. But before disappointment sets in, you note that the ball is tracking right at the hole. With its last turn, it tumbles, from the other side right into the jar. A misread and a mishit have conspired to become a birdie. Proving that Grandma was wrong—two wrongs can make a right—and that golf has space for luck, a sweet caprice that can bless our days.

❖

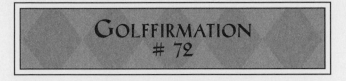

GOLFFIRMATION
72

A Blessing of Being Bad

YOU HAVE to love a game where frequent failure exalts occasional success. Surely, the pure pleasure of a mid-iron bounced just so onto the deck is enhanced by the pain of the two worm-burners that preceded it. Try to keep this in mind, if poor shots start to proliferate.

❖

GOLFFIRMATION
73

Walk a Mile in His Soft Spikes

THE PLAY-OFF at the 1989 Masters reveals all about the shared sympathies of golf. On the first hole, Scott Hoch, a world-class player who had achieved greatly but never broken through with a major title, had a two-foot putt to beat Nick Faldo. Hoch looked carefully, too carefully, at the putt, took his stance, and then backed away from a virtual tap-in! He circled it, paced the green, and took his time, turning the twenty-four inches into a journey.

Ben Crenshaw remembers watching on television from the clubhouse and dying for Hoch, as he watched golf disaster developing. "Oh, my God," he whispered. He wasn't alone. Indeed, in living rooms around the world, millions of golfers knew exactly what was happening to Hoch. The golf gremlins had him in their grip. His brain and body were at odds. His hopes and fears were short-circuiting the skill he had so finely honed. Finally, when Hoch stood over the mini-putt again and hit it, the ball bolted four feet past the hole. Faldo, given a reprieve, finished the wounded Hoch off with a twenty-footer for birdie on the next hole.

Golf makes a man tender and sympathetic, even through television. Golf enlarges your heart.

❖

The Secrets of Excess

SOMEONE'S FATHER used to say that you had to think like a hero just to be a decent human being. If you aimed really high, you might manage to achieve some reasonable level of performance.

The principle of exaggeration often works wonders in the game. If you have a habit of taking the club back inside, then to take it back straight from the ball, imagine you're taking it back a little *outside* the line. Similarly, if you have a habit of cutting off your swing, not finishing through the ball, then as you move through contact, imagine that you're a batter hitting a baseball to the opposite field. If the target line is noon, imagine you're throwing the club head toward one o'clock or even two. You'll end up driving straight through the ball.

❖

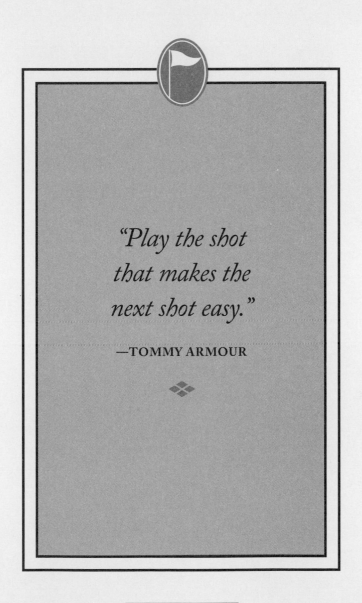

"*Play the shot
that makes the
next shot easy.*"

—TOMMY ARMOUR

You're Better than This Pro

 WHO AMONG us hasn't walked through the valley of golf despair? When things get their worst, console yourself with one name—Ray Ainsley.

Ainsley was playing in the 1938 U.S. Open at Cherry Hills Country Club in Denver when he hit his ball into a stream guarding the 16th hole. He could see the ball clearly under a few inches of water, so he decided to play it. Just as he was about to hit it, the current moved the ball. He flailed at the ball nine more times, until finally, on his 13th swing, he sent it flying into some bushes over the green. From there, it only took him three more blows to get it onto the green, and three putts for what still stands, sixty-four years later, as the highest single hole score ever registered in a professional golf championship: 19. Fifteen over par on one hole! Even money, you've never had a 19. Yeah, maybe 11, 12, or even 13. But take comfort that you've never pulled an Ainsley.

❖

GOLFFIRMATION
76

A Prayer for Practice Range Wisdom

CAST OUT, O Lord, the practice range temptation to thump balls aimlessly with my new diamond/beryllium driver. Banish the gorilla from my brain, the thirst for careless concussion.

Grant me instead the discipline to tutor my tune-up, to pick a target for each practice shot and absorb the feedback from the flight of same. Allow me the warm-up wisdom to work with my wedge and my short irons, too. Finally, dear Lord, inform my step. Guide me from the range to the practice green, the terrain of tap, the dance floor of small muscles and big results. I beseech you, O Lord, help me to actually practice that which may actually help me take a few bucks from good old Dave.

GOLFFIRMATION
77

The Power of Plain Persistence

YOU TOP your drive, skite your second, fat your third into the bunker left, then blast out—into the bunker right—and leave your 5th in the sand. Despair and self-loathing compete to fill your heart. Do not, repeat, *do not* pick up your ball and write down an X. Stay in the hole. Invent a new ambition—up and down from the bunker for 7. If you then blast back into bunker #1—hey, get up and down for a snowman.

If you don't finish, then you become a person who doesn't finish, and that's not the kind of person you are. You always finish. They can't stop you. You are a finisher.

❖

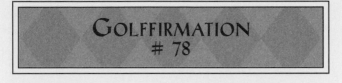

GOLFFIRMATION
78

Remembrance of Swings Past

SOME PHILOSOPHERS claim that the great tragedy of life is our inability to remember. And the reliably contrarian Mark Twain offered that the real tragedy is our inability to forget. But the golfer walks both tragic paths. Our brains won't let us remember the perfectly struck mid-iron that homed in the flag, stuck, and rolled three feet by. And it won't let us forget the fatted 3-iron that rolled twelve feet from point of contact and laughed at us from there. Somehow we must develop a selective memory. Forget our failures. And standing over a difficult shot, let us make a mental picture of the one exactly like it that we hit firm and true.

GOLFFIRMATION
79

Laugh, Clown, Laugh

Is THERE a game with more laughter in it than golf? True, our follies start out painful. The first-hole tee-ball that dents the cart is rarely amusing. But there often comes a point, late in a lost round or when the failure is so grotesque, that laughs become tonic.

Imagine, if you will, a brother-in-law (initials B. D.) hitting two sleeves into the pond fronting 13. Imagine further, that he did so in a staccato Chaplinesque vexation, despite the best efforts of his companions to get him to step away from the fire and take a breath.

Imagine that the instant the third ball left his clubface, he reached into his bag, pulled out three more balls, and dropped them on the fairway. He wanted to be ready for his fourth, fifth, and sixth. The Incident at Crumpin Pond brings smiles ten years later.

In golf, failure can be funny. True, his shank is funnier than yours. But beneath the discipline and attention the game requires, the antic lurks, ready to write comic legends. And most of us, eventually, get comfortable with our occasional comic incompetence.

❖

GOLFFIRMATION
80

When the Wheels Come Off

IT STRIKES like an assassin—suddenly and with deadly force. You're playing your usual game, managing some medium misses, cracking a good one now and then, when in a flash, your body forgets everything it's ever known about how to swing a club. You can't find the ball with the clubhead or sniff a rhythm. Your game is gone. You carded a snowman on 12, a double on 13, and suddenly, a grand day on the course is threatening to become an ordeal. The last five holes loom ahead, no longer a pleasure with friends, but an endless travail. Here's how to stop the bleeding on the next tee:

Put the driver away and pull out the 3-wood. Choke down on it and take a nice, gentle three-quarter flicking swing. Your ambition is to just put the ball in play in the fairway. Two hundred yards will be perfectly fine.

Come back an inch at a time.

❖

GOLFFIRMATION
81

Manners at Match Play

THE SCENE is Royal Birkdale, the Ryder Cup Championship in 1969. Jack Nicklaus and England's Tony Jacklin come to the 18th green with the Ryder Cup in the balance. Nicklaus putts first and makes a tricky putt to guarantee a tie. Jacklin's got a missable three-footer left, but in a remarkable act of sportsmanship, Nicklaus concedes the putt. Their match was halved, and so was The Ryder Cup match as a whole: 16–16. Since the United States held the cup at the time, they retained it, but lots of people, including some of Nicklaus' teammates, felt it was wrong. Nicklaus barely spoke of it, but clearly he respected Jacklin too much to put him in a position to lose the Ryder Cup by missing a short one. In a single move by the Golden Bear, we learn both the toughness of the game and the mercy at its heart.

❖

GOLFFIRMATION
82

Only Fools Play Winter Rules

SOME PEOPLE who play but don't understand golf, use what they call "winter rules." This betrayal of the game means you can roll the ball over in the fairway. If you're not happy with the lie, you can nudge the ball up onto a nice yeasty patch of grass. Don't ever do it. It doesn't matter if the fairway and greens are a mess, if they've been chewed up by hordes of exotic earthworms. Play the ball as it lays. Play it "down." Don't be touching it, turning it over, so everything is nice and easy. Let the game teach you something.

❖

Why We Play

YOU'VE DONE it. You have arranged your swing, or, rather, allowed your swing to happen so that right now the ball is ascending in a delicious parabolic arc. And you know, somehow you know, that this shot will be close. The only question—as the ball, etched against the sky, starts to drop, sweetly, strongly toward its destination—is how close. In that moment, elation is inevitable. The cares of all else fall away and you feel happy, just stupid, silly, happy. Savor the moment.

❖

GOLFFIRMATION
84

Early Birdies

JEROME TRAVERS won the U.S. Amateur four times and even won the U.S. Open in 1915. But his greatest achievement may be this quote that ranks golf as important as love: "In golf, as in other sports, youth is a great helper, but if you cannot start at three, or twelve, or even thirty-five, start at forty-five or fifty. Remember it is better to have golfed and foozled, than never to have golfed at all."

The Blessing of Birdies
That Might Have Been

IT LANDED ten feet past the hole,
And backed up, baby, bless my soul.
It thought of dropping, perhaps an ace.
But settled below, from the cup, a pace.

Yet as you walk toward green with hope,
The taste of dread grows in your throat.
Doubt and worry tease your brain,
What if you miss? becomes refrain.

You won't miss this, comes back reply,
You're a player, a stud, a birdie guy.
Thirty inches, straight up the hill,
Just firm the surlyn dimpled pill.

Don't flinch or yip or think of missing,
Just strike it true, all doubt dismissing.
Play dead center, nice and cool.
Don't read a break. Be bold, you fool.

You take your stance and start your blade,
But in that nanosecond, you gulp, afraid.
Your putter somehow hits the turf,
You make a murmured sound like *Erf.*

And as the ball starts rolling, no, sliding,
Time itself, it starts dividing.
You'd sell your son to rewind the spool,
If only mullies on the green were cool.

Yet it looks as though it's center cut.
You could get lucky and make this putt.
But when the ball just stops, two inches shy.
For a moment, you think you might actually cry.

But even tears can't ease the pain,
Of having no heart, no guts, no brain.
Of suddenly knowing you're not man, but chimp,
Sans cojones, a feckless wimp.

The ball just sits there, spewing invective,
Idiot, weasel, mental defective.
It cruelly mocks your every failing,
Cholesterol, career, that teenage jailing.

The ball just glistens not in the cup.
It's stopped moving, not in, and God
    help you, never up.
Your playing partners avert their eyes.
A trio of *but-for-the-grace-of-God-go-I*s.

They offer naught for words of balm,
Are kindly mute, in brotherly psalm.
They've been there, done that, have their stories,
Of putts left short and thwarted glories.

They say that pain expands our heart,
Make us deep and good, soul-smart,
Kind and caring, gracious, tender,
Susceptible to all God's splendor.

So, in desperate search of growth, let us pray,
That there's hope in every golf misplay.
That God enhances and softens our soul,
For every birdie that dies below the hole.

❖

GOLFFIRMATION
86

Chase Like Arnie

PALMER HAD the personality of a champion and one swing trait that might help your game resemble his ever so slightly. Nobody chased the ball "out of there" like Arnie. As he came through the ball, you could almost sense him keeping the clubhead low and powerful, and on line as long as anatomically possible. There's a feeling of his clubhead pursuing the ball down the line. And his characteristic low finish pointed the club directly toward the target as though telling the ball where it was to go. Stay down and through, and chase the ball out of there. If indecision infects your swing, remember, finish through it like Arnie. While you're at it, enjoy the energy of the attack the way he did, too.

❖

GOLFFIRMATION
87

*Of Building the World
and Building a Swing*

ANDREW CARNEGIE knew something about success. He built the steel industry, which means he's responsible for . . . well, just about everything. He understood both capitalism and golf's power. That's why he called our game "an indispensable adjunct of civilization."

❖

GOLFFIRMATION
88

A Lesson from a Legend

FOR ALL you need to know about the importance of grip, alignment, and stance consider
the wisdom of Jim Flick, one of the great
teachers of the game: "Most of the things that con-
tribute to a bad shot in golf occur before you begin
your backswing."

❖

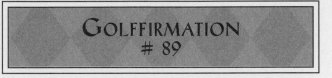

GOLFFIRMATION
89

Further Proof that God Loves Golfers

IT IS a tribute to the game's greatness that the tale of Ted Barnhouse could conceivably be true. According to *The Golf Nut's Book of Amazing Feats and Records,* when cattleman Barnhouse teed it up on the 4th hole at Mountain View Country Club in Oregon, he shanked his drive over a fence into a field and off the skull of a cow. From there, it hit a sprinkler head, bounced off a parked lawn mower near the green, rolled toward the hole, and banged into the flagstick, before disappearing for an ace. Amen.

❖

GOLFFIRMATION
90

Frailty, Thy Name Is Golfer

ENGLISHMAN BERNARD DARWIN is widely considered the first of the great golf scribes. He summed up a fundamental and inspiring golf truth thusly: "If I miss a shot, a drive, an iron shot, or whatever it may be, I do not catechize myself as to what I did wrong or wonder if I shall do it wrong again next time; I simply accept this miss as an inevitable result of being a very frail and ordinary mortal." Alas, though such equanimity may forever exceed our grasp, Darwin's humility is an achievement to which we can all aspire.

❖

A Limerick Fix

A DOCTOR named David yanked left.
In the deep rough he was often bereft.
He moved back the ball,
Just a smidge, that was all,
And from fairway, he was often quite deft.

His brother, young Phil, was reversed.
His short irons went right, he seemed cursed.
But when he moved the ball up,
His wedges sought the cup,
And in pars he became quite well versed.

❖

GOLFFIRMATION
92

Be Narrow-Minded

ALMOST ALL golfers who struggle to break 90—or even 100—share a weakness. They forget to aim precisely, in Harvey Penick's famous phrase to "take dead aim." They never focus on *precisely* where they want the ball to go. So pick out a teeny, tiny target—not just the left side of the green or fifteen feet right of the flag or a ball on the high side, but a truly small bull's-eye. On a drive, it's the tip of that top branch. On a putt, it's the particular half-inch sliver of the hole over which the ball will dive into darkness. Targeting will help your mental game, too.

"A golfer needs to have something on his mind if he does not want thoughts about swing mechanics to intrude on his consciousness just as he is preparing to play his shot," quoth sports psychologist Dr. Bob Rotella. "The target helps fill that void. It helps prevent distraction."

GOLFFIRMATION
93

On Charming the Ball

ONCE WE'VE sent the ball on its way, most of us start yakking. We yelp "Get up" or "Sit down" or "Turn over" or "Bounce for me, baby." Sometimes we shout; sometimes we cajole; most often we beg. Rumor has it that some untutored players even become profane. But if profanity could change trajectory, surely scores would be lower.

Now Slammin' Sam Snead, the man believed to have the smoothest golf swing in history, had a different approach. He'd talk to his ball before launch. "This isn't going to hurt a bit," he'd tell the ball under his breath. "Sambo is just going to give you a nice little ride." Or "Hello, Dimples, I see you're sitting up fat and ready; let us have some fun." So as you settle in behind the ball, heed Snead's advice: "By acting as if the ball is human, I distract myself, leaving no time for thoughts of this and that. Get charming with your golf ball if you want pars and birdies."

❖

GOLFFIRMATION
94

Feelin' Groovy

 EVERYTHING ABOUT which you care matters. Consider the small, pristine pleasure in cleaning your grooves. Whether it's a gentle night-before scrubbing with a soft wire brush, or a fairway reaming with the point of a tee, maintaining those small canals, the source of precious spin, is an act of stewardship. Take pride. Be careful. There is no such thing as a small advantage.

❖

GOLFFIRMATION
95

Every Shot Makes Someone Happy

O LORD, help me see the error of my joy when my opponent shanks his approach shot into the tool shed. Allow me to understand that my little happy dance—done, of course, behind his back—is wrong. And further help me to lift up my heart, to not thrill at the sight of his ball rolling off the green into the pond or at the sound of his ball whocking into a stand of birch trees. Oh, most of all, Lord, let my heart be compassionate instead of giddy with delight, when my beloved brother, my companion of all my days, whiffs. Keep me from giggling with pleasure.

❖

GOLFFIRMATION
96

Unexpected Elations

"FOR MOST people—even the most frantic and least peaceful players—there are sublime moments on the course, mini-enlightenments. These might come after a great shot or a thrilling victory, but they might also descend upon us for no apparent reason as we walk the eleventh fairway in a light wind, stand on the first tee at dawn, or drive our cart up the little rise near the 18th green when the sun is about to set, the flagstick casts a long shadow, and the windows of the clubhouse glow in the dusk. These moments are golf's little gifts to us. The real value of them, perhaps the real value of golf, lies in the vision they afford us of our best selves, our capacity for peace."

– *Roland Merullo,* A Passion for Golf

❖

GOLFFIRMATION
97

The Flagstick Is a Figment

IT'S HARD for the high-handicapper to resist flag-hunting. You've busted a tee-ball down the middle. You've got 135 left to a front pin, tucked behind a bunker. Your brain tells you to aim for the center of the green. But your longing cries out for you to fire a dart. "You can do it," temptation whispers. "Remember? Seven years ago in Virginia? You were playing with your dad, and you flat stuck an 8-iron over a pond four feet from the pin."

Try to resist the siren call, the allure of the spectacular shot. Lots of the greatest golfers in our history have made fortunes aiming for the center of the green. And guess what? Now and then your aim will be off and a tap-in will result. Don't play yourself out of a match. Be patient. Wait for genuine opportunity. Jim McLean, one of the great teachers, suggests imagining that there is no pin. Learn to make the middle of the green your home.

❖

GOLFFIRMATION
98

Of Lycra and the Long Ball

BABE DIDRIKSON ZAHARIAS was one of the greatest woman golfers in history. She also had the drink-deep, go-for-the-gusto personality of that other Babe: Babe Ruth. When asked the secret to hitting the ball so far, she got to the simple truth: "Just loosen your girdle and let the ball have it." Remember Babe, when you forget to be strong through the ball.

On Camaraderie and Why We Play

 MICHAEL MURPHY'S classic, *Golf in the Kingdom,* tells the final tender truth about golf:

So Agatha spoke about golf and about the love men have for one another. "It's the only reason ye play at all," she said. "It's a way ye've found to get togither and yet maintain a proper distance. I know you men. Yer not like women or Italians, huggin' and embracin' each other. Ye need tae feel yer separate love . . . All those gentlemanly rools, why, they're proper rools of affection—all the waitin' and oohin' and aahin' o'er yer shots, all the talk o' this one's drive and that one's putt and the other one's gorgeous swing—what is it all but love? Men lovin' men, that's what golf is."

❖

GOLFFIRMATION # 100

Why We Play

EACH GOLF swing is a snowflake—one of a kind. Your brother's is that wicked lash, your son's a syrupy swoop. Greg's got the tomahawk chop, and Dan that giant loop. Consider that from hundreds of yards away, across a foggy fairway, we can identify the man by his singular move through the ball. We all struggle to follow the same rules and yet dazzle in our diversity.

GOLFFIRMATION
101

Golfers Beware

"NEVER BET anyone with his name stenciled on his bag. Never bet anyone who carries a 1-iron. Never bet anyone with a deep tan but whose left hand is the color of mayonnaise. Never bet a guy named 'Chick' . . . If a stranger offers you a stroke a hole, decline. If he's a right-hander and offers to play you left-handed, or vice versa, beg off. If he proposes a series of bets requiring audio-visual aids to explain, pass. And if a guy offers to play you with just a putter, or with a rake and a shovel, or a Dr. Pepper bottle taped to a stick, do not bet this man."

— *Jon Winokur*

❖

GOLFFIRMATION
102

A Gripping Tale

ALL THE great teachers preach the importance of the grip. If the linkage between man and tool is imprecise the work is rarely fine. But remember another linkage, too—the connection between the length of your backswing and what happens to your grip at the top. According to Tommy Armour, a world-class competitor and teaching pro at the Boca Raton Club in Florida for twenty-five years, the most serious common error at the top of the swing is the loosening of the left-hand grip. If your backswing is too big, your left hand of necessity lets go. When you feel it, you panic, and hit from the top, with the right hand. Nothing good can come of that. When you feel like you're losing your grip, remember that the whole world is in your hands. Try taking a smaller swing.

❖

GOLFFIRMATION
103

Faith Leads to Pars

FAITH NOT only moves mountains, it lowers scores. Remember the wisdom of golf psychologist Dr. Bob Rotella: "It is more important to be decisive than to be correct when preparing to play any golf shot . . ."

❖

Humility Marks Us as Men

FOR THE suburban golfer in need of salve for his wounds, the history of the 17th hole at St. Andrew's, called the Road Hole, offers a consoling catalog of professional golfer incompetence. Often cited as the single hardest hole on earth, the 461-yard, par-4 has brought the world's greatest golfers to grief. More than a century ago, a player named David Ayton got to the Road Hole with a 5-shot lead in the British Open. He was a hundred feet from the hole in 2; he took an 11 and didn't take the claret jug. More recently, in 1978, Tommy Nakajima's hopes for a British Open title died on the green at 17.

Nakajima was safely on the deck in two. But when he tapped his first putt, he watched it take an unexpected left turn and trundle on down to the bottom of the pot bunker left of the green. The man from Japan descended into the Celtic cairn and swung once, twice, three times before he even got the ball out of the well. He then chipped it back to 2-putt position, whence it had come 5 strokes ago. Two strokes later, he was in for a quintuple bogey, snowman plus one, a.k.a. 9. Bye-bye, British Open.

The moral of the story? Don't hate yourself for what happened on 15 today. Don't wallow in self-loathing. Accept the lash, soldier. Keep moving. It's what we do after we get knocked down that measures us as men.

❖

GOLFFIRMATION
105

Please Welcome the Reigning Dub

IN AUGUST 1988 Jeff Sluman joined an elite fraternity when he won the PGA Championship at Oak Tree Golf Club in Edmond, Oklahoma. Shortly thereafter he was on the first tee at the world series of golf, and found himself taking pride in being presented to the gallery, for the first time, as the PGA champion. He stepped up to his ball and proceeded to dub a drive forty yards in the general direction of the hole. One beauty of the game is its reliable ruthlessness. The next time you follow a pretty par with a grounder to short off the next tee, remember that golf tests us all. Find your ball. Hit it again.

❖

GOLFFIRMATION
106

The 19th Hole

No MATTER the results, there is pleasure in the coming home. The clattering into the clubhouse, the refreshments, cold and carbonated, the crisp and salty, and above all the gab—the lamentations, the if-onlys, the confessions of shanks and lurches, the simple satisfaction of having made it through. There is always victory in enduring, in finishing the task. And friendship blooms amid the satisfactions of the folks we've traveled with. We have borne witness to each other's follies and strengths, seen the secret sides of each other's souls.

❖

GOLFFIRMATION
107

*There Is No Rattlesnake
Beneath the Ball*

LORD, BANISH the brute from my soul. Teach me to accept that there's not a poisonous snake under my ball, and so, there is no reason to chop violently downward with a spastic lurch, to bury my clubhead three inches into the topsoil, as one might were one trying to kill a serpent about to strike.

❖

GOLFFIRMATION
108

Aim for Hues

THE GAMES gets flavored by the seasons. For the autumn golfer, the trees in the distance become targets. Though in summer, they're indistinguishable from afar, in October in Vermont, the shades of foliage make the golden tree—or maybe it's flame-orange—your line of flight. Use nature's bounty, and while you're at it, aspire to be impressed by the tumult of the colors. Beauty is the backbeat of the game.

❖

GOLFFIRMATION
109

Better to Be Lucky than Good

WINNING ON the PGA Tour always requires skill and often requires luck. If you doubt it, consider the caprice that helped Roger Maltbie win the 1976 Memorial Tournament at Muirfield Village in Ohio. He was in a playoff with Hale Irwin when he walloped a drive that was clearly headed out of bounds. This would have cost him stroke and distance. But because it was Maltbie's turn to win, the ball actually hit one of the white stakes marking out-of-bounds and bounced back in play. Maltbie went on to win and took that o.b. stake with him and carried it in his bag for a while. In the moments that your errant drive is flying toward disaster, console yourself with Maltbie's white stake. It's possible, just possible, that yours will hit a bobcat and carom back into play.

❖

GOLFFIRMATION
110

An Invitation to Tee

THE GOLF tee may be the very embodiment of welcome. "Here," sayeth the slim wooden peg, "allow me to make this easy for you. Allow me to hold the ball in such a way as to accommodate your swing. Is there any device in life more simply versatile? A touch higher perhaps, sir, for a high flying ball? Or perhaps lower, to help a 3-iron cheat the wind?" The simple shapely generosity of the golf tee is not to be overlooked. It makes life ready for you.

That's worth appreciating.

❖

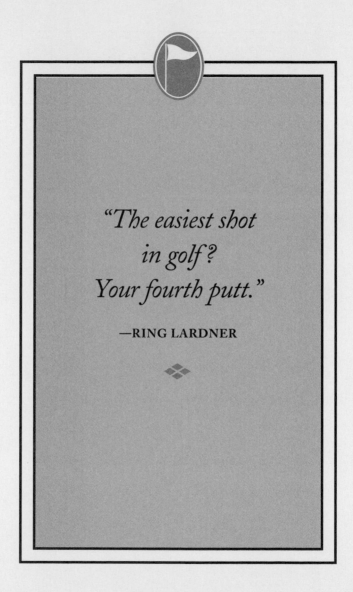

*"The easiest shot
in golf?
Your fourth putt."*

—RING LARDNER

Why We Play

ALISTAIR COOKE was a British journalist and terrific golf writer before he achieved fame in the United States as the host of PBS's *Masterpiece Theatre*. He managed to pinpoint one of the darker allures of the game. "Golf," he said, "was just what the Scottish character had been seeking for centuries, namely, a method of self-torture."

So, when your own performance is less than stellar, write off the round as contrition for your venial sins. You're a good man, but you can be better—don't you think?

❖

GOLFFIRMATION
112

We Happy Few, We Band of Brothers

A MAN has seven brothers. Two of them are genetic brothers. Some have married his sisters. But all are tied by a bond stronger than DNA or plighted troth—golf. Each year, they travel together to the great gentle mountains of Maine in search of what? Self-discipline? A single smooth 7-iron? Or is it fraternity?

For three days they set forth onto the fairways, united in hope, enriched by their willingness to fail in front of each other. They compete for the most important golf championship in the world—the only major Tiger will never win—the Martindale Classic. And while chasing the trophy, they laugh, taunt each other, brag, celebrate, mourn, get some exercise and some sun, and make some memories. A whiff has been stored in the historical files, as have long irons that split the pin. Stupid and sweet and determined and dumb and daring, they are united by history, exalted by the blood they share.

❖

GOLFFIRMATION
113

The Golfer's Goodnight

Now I lay me down to sleep,
To count some birdies, instead of sheep.
As I slip into the land of Nod,
Prepare me for the morrow, God.

Inform my trunk with fullish turn,
To thwart those shots that earthworms burn.
Imbue my soul with supple ease,
Spare me snowmen, Lord, oh please.

Banish thoughts like lurch and whack,
And don't let my tee-ball hit the halfway shack.
Subtract the tension from my mind,
And grant me the luck to stray shots find.

As I drift off into rest,
Give me the love to meet the test.
Help me to enjoy my fellows,
The course, the trees, the autumn yellows,

The grass, the air, your vault of sky.
Save me from excess of try.
Teach me to savor every swing,
And to remember, that to play's the thing.

❖

GOLFFIRMATION
114

Uphill Shorties

IN A game replete with heartbreak, few rival the short uphill putt that stops three inches shy of the hole. Here's an image that will help you stop babying the ball. Imagine that there's a small wall curving around the back half of the hole. Have faith and firm it. The wall will deflect anything hit too firmly right back into the bottom. If you're uncertain with the shorties, you leave too much to chance.

❖

GOLFFIRMATION
115

In the Land of Golf,
Even Bad Is Good

GOLF IS so generous that it offers special gifts to those who are most needy. Here's novelist George Plimpton on a high side for high handicappers:

> Naturally the bad golfer sees much more terrain than the expert. He has the greater opportunity, should he be so inclined, to indulge in horticultural, or even ornithological, practice. His chances are far greater than the professional's of running into a chestnut-sided warbler, for example, which is shy and tends to flit around in the lower branches of heavy shrubbery, familiar duffer's territory. The good golfer rarely has a chance at this sort of thing.

❖

GOLFFIRMATION
116

Of Cuckoo Clocks and Kings

P. G. WODEHOUSE captured the humbling democracy of the game: "Like some capricious goddess, golf bestows its favours with an almost fat-headed lack of method or discrimination. On every side, we see big two-fisted he-men floundering around in three figures, stopping every few minutes to let through little shrimps with knock knees and hollow cheeks who are tearing off snappy seventy-fours. Giants of finance have to accept a stroke a hole from their junior clerks. Men capable of governing empires fail to control a small white ball, which presents no difficulties whatever to others without one ounce more brain than a cuckoo clock."

❖

On Stopping Topping

WHEN YOU'VE grown weary of hitting only the top three dimples, try to keep this down-and-through image from Englishman Henry Cotton in the forefront of your brain.

"Imagine that the ball has little legs," said the three-time British Open champion, "and chop them off."

❖

GOLFFIRMATION
118

A Meditation for Wisdom in the Woods

OKAY, YOU'RE in the lumber, Paul Bunyan. But, no big deal. Think damage control. Just punch it out into the fairway, get it back into play, and you're still in the hole. You're looking good for bogey and who knows? You slap a nice 7-iron up there with your third, get lucky, and drop a putt. You might make par yet.

But then you see it . . . the temptation . . . the opening . . . a twelve-foot wide opportunity between those two trees up ahead. And framed by the trees is the flag, shining like a beacon on top of the hill. Maybe, just maybe, you think, if you hit a screaming low-liner, keep it under the leaves, and clear the crest, you might, just maybe, be able to run one up onto the green.

There are, of course, a few problems. First, you'd have to hit the ball with the precision of a ballistic missile, controlling both its line of flight and its trajectory, a skill which you have never—not once, in over twenty-two years of greens fees—demonstrated.

Two, your ball is nestled behind a tree root, sitting in what appears to be the hoofprint of a New Mexican mule deer. Still, the spirit of what-if beckons. A birdie from the heart of darkness—that seems worth wanting. A story to tell the boys.

"What would Tiger do?" you ask yourself.

"I'm not Tiger," you ought to reply.

But in that moment you somehow imagine that you are. You hear the shouts from the crowd as your ball zips under the leaves, splits the trees, mounts the hill, and rockets toward the green, running, running, through the fringe and settling at last, amid the thunderous roar, four feet below the hole.

And so inspired, you take your stance and prepare to meet destiny. You hood a 4-iron and hit it, somehow, dead solid. One problem: The ball hits a tree dead solid as well and bounces back and hits you above the left eye, dropping at your feet. A beat later, you fall on top of it. With a 2-stroke penalty you're lying 4, in as tight a jail as you were before. You're also in pain, with a not-trivial trickle of blood dripping down from your brow, obscuring your vision for shot number 5.

Lord, hear my prayer. Help me to take my medicine, to understand that I'm not Tiger. Teach me to love and respect the limited and honest golfer that I am.

❖

GOLFFIRMATION
119

Time to Look

GOLF SLOWS life down—a good thing, these days. "The pace of living is so fast today," said Jackie Burke Sr., who endured the heartbreak of losing the 1920 U.S. Open by a single shot, "that a golf course is one of the last places to watch a squirrel climb a tree."

Look for squirrels.

❖

GOLFFIRMATION
120

Let's Not Make a Deal

O LORD, teach me the wisdom not to nego-
tiate with you. Help me to understand that I
shouldn't promise to do years of charity work
if only you'll, what—let my drive somehow find the
short grass, or guide this twenty-footer for birdie to
the bottom of the cup. Give me the clarity to appreciate that such deals are both morally wrong and extremely bad strategy. Lift up my heart to accept that
confidence in my stroke is a better tool than merely
begging for your mercy.

❖

GOLFFIRMATION
121

When You're Down and Troubled

AN ANNOYING old adage advises the afflicted to keep in mind that someone always has it worse than you do. For the golfer, the suffering of others is rarely balm. But perhaps there's small comfort, and a chuckle, in George Plimpton's claim that his longtime editor Joe Fox—a brilliant publisher, but less than gifted golfer—once hit a golf ball between his own legs. So however you play, you're more like Tiger than you are like Fox.

❖

Death Be Not Par

CHI CHI RODRIGUEZ gets close to the exquisite anxiety. Death did not frighten him at all, he said, but three-footers for par, those were another matter. The sagacious Sam Snead made the same point with an adventure story. "I shot a wild elephant in Africa thirty yards from me, and it didn't hit the ground until it was right at my feet," he said. "I wasn't scared a bit. But a four-foot putt scares me to death."

❖

GOLFFIRMATION
123

The Wonders of Stuff

 You're in one of those giant sporting-goods stores. You blow by the basketball aisle, the baseball stuff, all that running equipment, turn a corner, and, suddenly, there it is, laid out before you like a land of dreams—the golf section. No, make that the golf cornucopia. It's a glittery effusion of hope, a pleasure dome of clubs and shoes and balls and gloves, and maybe more important than things you might actually need, a slew of gadgets you—for no good reason—want.

"Look," the pilgrim enthuses, "here's a log for recording info about my putts"—ah, of course, the putting diary. That's the secret! That's the answer! "And look there, a device that will hold my golf tees smartly in parallel rows. Surely, that chaotic jumble in my bag pouch has been undermining the serenity I seek for my swing." From groove-cleaners to head-covers, from videotapes to training aids, we're addled by the vast vulgar ingenuity of capitalism. Useless

stuff is arrayed before fools and we want. That's all—
we want. Why? Who knows. Or content yourself
with the poet's non-explanation: The heart has its
reasons, the reason knows not of.

But know this of our longing. It isn't avaricious or
greedy. We're as innocent as lambs. We want because
we hope—to be better golfers, that is. And hope
makes us human.

❖

GOLFFIRMATION
124

Of Home Runs and Handicaps

FOR ALL you need to know about the difficulty of the game, consider this thought from no less an athlete than Hank Aaron, he of the 755 career home runs. "It took me seventeen years to get three thousand hits in baseball. I did it in one afternoon on the golf course."

❖

GOLFFIRMATION
125

The Longest Shot of All

A TWENTY-YEAR-OLD amateur from outside Boston gets credit for making golf the part of the American dream that it is today. Francis Ouimet modestly entered the 1913 U.S. Open held at the Country Club in Brookline, Massachusetts, a course where he had caddied while coming of age. Somehow, this golf cipher got into a play-off and prevailed over the two greatest players of the time, British professionals Harry Vardon and Ted Ray. Here's Ouimet on the moment he stood over the final putt: "I couldn't get my breath. The green began heaving beneath me. I couldn't even see the hole."

The story of David slaying the two Goliaths spread like a prairie fire, exalting red-white-and-blue pride and delighting every American who had a taste for the impossible.

❖

GOLFFIRMATION
126

A Televised Tranquilizer

IT'S 4:30 on a spring Saturday afternoon. A man has worked his yard a bit, perhaps pulled some weeds, pruned a branch here and there— tended his patch, however humble. He arrives in front of the television, sweaty and satisfied, carrying a glass of ice water, pops on the third round of, what—it could be the Masters, or it could be the Compaq Classic. The venue matters not. But, instantly, into his home comes the sweep of the greensward, the reliable hushed commentaries of reporters in towers, and the familiar lingo of birdies and buried lies. A feeling of well-being comes over the man. He feels contented having done his part and serene in the knowledge that the world has time for so civilized a game. A man with a clicker and a tournament on the tube has no need of liquor or meditation. He possesses inner peace, secure in the knowledge that, in the end, all shall be well.

GOLFFIRMATION
127

A Limerick Fix

WHEN A priest named Brian had a hook,
He found no answer in the Good Book.
But bottom-hand turned toward hole,
Front foot back, bless my soul,
And the cleric his flock's money took.

❖

GOLFFIRMATION
128

A Metaphor with a Motor

EVERYBODY'S LOOKING for the phrase that will inspire, the just-so combination of words that will turn the feel of a genuine golf swing into a reality. Here's a good one from the man with the swing many call the smoothest ever. "I try to feel oily," said the great Snead.

❖

Choose Your Weapon Wisely

YOU'RE STANDING proudly over your perfect drive. You've got 158 to the flag. Before you choose a tool for your approach shot, remember this from Henry Longhurst, cracking good player and cracking good golf journalist: "The mistake made by innumerable club golfers is that they tend to take a club with which they could reach the flag—if they hit their best shot with it. . . . If we hit thirty balls with the 7-iron, the vast majority will land in a square fifteen yards deep and twenty yards wide, and one will be out there on its own—fifteen yards ahead on any of its brethren. That one is the danger.

When clubbing yourself, pay no attention to the practice range shot that flew "painlessly off the club." Yes, you have the ability somewhere inside you, to hit a 7-iron that far. But choose your stick assuming the shot will be one of the big bunch of balls in the middle.

GOLFFIRMATION
130

The Pleasures of Impossible

WHENEVER GOOD men talk about the great golf courses of the world, Pine Valley gets plenty of palaver. It's not only a physically distinctive course, located in the scrubby, sandy, and oddly beautiful pine barrens of Clementon, New Jersey—it's also an extremely difficult track. Countless passable players with handicaps in the teens have been forced to beg for mercy. So great is the legend of punitive Pine Valley that it's tough to separate the true disaster stories from the apocryphal.

Golf writer Bernard Darwin is said to have been even par through seven holes and to have quit when he took a 16 on the 8th. There's a famously deep bunker on the par-3 10th hole, from which men are reported to have carded single-hole scores in the 20s. Lots of first-timers gripe like little babies that the course is just way too harsh on shots that are off by just a whisker. But writer Peter Dobereiner got it right about Pine Valley, and indeed anything that's not easy, when he said of the horror tales:

> They only tell the lesser half of the story. Because of the perils which beset the golfer on every side, the charge of exhilaration he receives when he successfully carries his drive over 170 yards of sandy waste is proportionately increased. The hitting of a green, a routine enough experience at your home club, becomes a thrill. And as for holing across those undulating greens with surfaces as slick as polished marble, watching the ball swing as much as twenty feet on its roller-coaster route, the afterglow of achievement lasts for weeks. So, while playing Pine Valley can be a penance, and nearly always is, somewhere during the round, the agonies are the price which must be paid for the ecstasies.

Now, there's a man who understands both games—golf and the other one.

❖

GOLFFIRMATION
131

Presidential Golf

LOTS OF our topkicks have loved the game: Harding, Eisenhower, Kennedy, Nixon, Ford, Bush, Clinton, and Bush the Younger. But the ultimate endorsement comes from the portly William Howard Taft: "[Golf] should be indulged in when the opportunity arises, as every man who has played the game knows that it rejuvenates and stretches the span of life."

GOLFFIRMATION
132

No Gimmes

THE TRUE golfer has the same disdain for gimmes that he does for mulligans and for winter rules. It's simple: All balls go in the hole. Even the ones hanging on the lip. Unless, of course, they don't matter. If it's match play, and you're in for par, go right ahead and give the fellow his putt for bogey. But if the result of the stroke matters, it's vital to the spirit of the game that every stroke be played. A gimme suggests that putts can't be missed. Enough said.

If you take putts or give them, you undermine the beautiful rigor of golf. Sam Snead offered some good life advice: "Keep close count of your nickels and dimes, stay away from whiskey, and never concede a putt."

❖

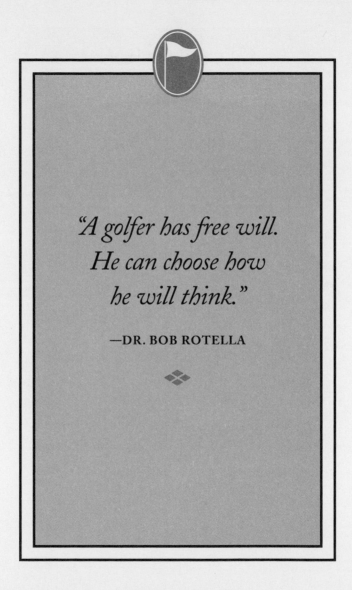

"*A golfer has free will.*
He can choose how
he will think."

—DR. BOB ROTELLA

GOLFFIRMATION
133

Don't Get Mad, Stay Even

No LESS a figure that England's King George V put it thusly: "Golf always makes me so damned angry." We've all played with golfers who struggle with temper. They hit a flub or two, and they're so disappointed or frustrated or ashamed that they lose it. Often club abuse ensues; sometimes imprecations are sent heavenward. But if you watch the best on television, you'll see remarkable self-control. The *magnificos* of the game have learned to manage their emotions. "Golf has ingrained in them," wrote Tom Boswell, "a fierce restraint, a low-flame moderation, a constant acceptance of failure that is almost a religious vow."

As your temper flares, remember, the winner always stays calm.

❖

In Praise of the Hunter

(with apologies to Robert Frost)

THESE WOODS are lovely, dark, and deep.
A place that puts your hopes to sleep.
Your ball came in here, that you know.
You stumble through bramble, you startle a doe.
But searching for your errant shot,
A single clue you haven't got.

It could be in a knot-hole up a tree
Or 'neath a fern, oh woe is thee.
You crash through branches, into burrows peek,
Hmm, interesting bird—big yellow beak.

As you grope and crash, midst fauna and flora,
See if you can "feel" the ball's aura.
Survey the earth, that gully, this mound,
Something there is in a ball that wants
        to be found.

GOLFFIRMATION
135

Good Grooming Matters, Too

GOLF IS surely the most fashionable sport. From the dapper Hagen in the 1920s to most of the millions on public courses today, golfers choose their clothes just so. Of course, the choices aren't always good. But what matters isn't the combination of colors, but the deliberation, the care with which we prepare to go forth. "Golf is a game of rhythm, style, grace, not brute strength. It is a meticulous game," said sportswriter Jim Murray, "best played by persons who are neat."

When you get a television close-up of the golf shoes on the best players in the game, they're always detailed and polished to a high shine. True, they were buffed by the clubhouse staff, not the player. But the attention those shoes celebrate insinuates its way into the swings. Promise yourself to dress carefully, to present yourself with pride. Shined shoes are good for at least a stroke a side.

❖

We're Gonna Go Through It Together

YOU'RE PLAYING with a friend of twenty years. He's known you since you both were boys in, where was it—the Bronx? The bayou? He's helped you through . . . well, everything. And you've done just fine as a friend, too. A minute ago you both split the fairway with tee-balls for all time, and now you're on the way to certain birdies. Side by side, under God's heaven, golf gives you an excuse to walk, and talk, and laugh and just be near each other, in sunshine and in shadow.

Let fellowship make the day a pleasure.

❖

GOLFFIRMATION
137

A Certain Wit

 GOLF CAN make you a wonderful sort of wise guy. It steeps a brutal frankness into your soul. For example, when Mark Brooks, the winner of the 1996 PGA Championship, was asked to describe a four-putt in the U.S. Open, he said, "One, two, three, four."

❖

GOLFFIRMATION
138

Of Men and Memories

IT'S OFTEN noted that people who are forgetful in many matters—most often men—have flawless memories when it comes to golf shots. As one wife, whose wedding anniversary had gone unmarked, put it: "How is it possible to remember the exact spot from which your opponent hit his third shot two years ago on the 16th hole, and forget the date on which I made a dreadful mistake of committing to you until death us do part?" Fair question, to which we do not know the answer. But we do know it has nothing to do with a lack of love for our wives. It has far more to do with the neural pathways of our brains. Exactly what it has to do with the neural pathways of our brains, we have no clue. We're just blessed, that's all—and grateful for the gift.

Never apologize for the magic of a golf memory.

❖

Advice for Both Golf and Life

WE ALL know the sports metaphor for getting to any life goal. You've got to keep your eye on the ball, right? Yes, but apparently, that's not enough when it comes to golf. Or so says the man with more insight into the game than all other men. According to Arnold Haultain, it's not enough to merely look at the ball with your peepers: "You must 'look' with the most concentrated and absorbed attention. A casual or half-hearted look is suicidal. And you must look with the mind's eye as well as with the sensory one—and the one must be as keen, as clear, and as alert as the other."

❖

Death to the Mulligan

O LORD, grant me the courage to resist the mulligan. Help me to see that the first shot of the day is in many ways the hardest one of all, and that accepting a do-over betrays the game we love and turns it into something, well . . . easier than golf. Help me to understand that the game's moral beauty lies in its difficulty, and in the simple plainness that every stroke counts—not just the ones we like. Lord, help me understand that if I take mulligans, I might as well never turn in a score, might as well give up the game, take up something more forgiving, like tennis or maybe watching television.

Lord, help me to understand that the old joke has it right. An American, playing his first round in Scotland, scuffs his first tee-ball, tees up another, and stripes it down the middle. He turns to his Scottish playing partner and says, "In the States, we call that a mulligan. What do you call it here?" The Scot, heading down the fairway, replies with the truth, "Three."

GOLFFIRMATION
141

Amen

FRENCH PHILOSOPHER Simone Weil once said that any undivided attention is prayer. Question: Is there anything in life to which people give more focused attention than their golf games? The game calls forth our humanity, and according to one smart French woman, is deeply spiritual.

❖

Get Thee to the Practice Green

 OF COURSE, you like to whack the ball,
The arc can be inspiring.
A wedge or driver struck just so
Sets adrenal glands to firing.

But get thee to the practice green,
My friend, to make the grade.
For 40 of your 90 shots
Will be stricken with the blade.

The 3-iron, you'll hit twice all day,
Wedges, you might strike ten.
But the flat stick, whatever happens,
You'll hit over and over again.

Get thee to the practice green.
Work on focus and repetition.
Notice where you're missing, friend,
Small adjustments are your mission.

Sure, hit a bucket, loosen up,
And groove that swing in prep.
But don't forget the small strokes, pal,
They'll help you win your bet.

Get thee to the practice green,
Don't be a driving range dummy.
The moss is where your game will learn
To take your buddy's money.

❖

GOLFFIRMATION
143

The Wonderful Word Wallop

"SWING EASY" is a common correction for a golfer who gets lost. And yet, as always with our sinister subtle game, there is danger for the dub who gets delicate. For somewhere in a fluid, well-tempoed swing must come a moment of abandon, an instant—between the time when the club is hip-high on the way down and hip-high on your follow-through—where inhibition gives way to the authority of a forceful pass through the ball.

The secret is finding the elusive balance between excessive exertion and not enough. But in the bottom half of the circle that is your swing, remember a word we don't hear enough today: *wallop*. Just don't start walloping too soon. Consider this nugget from the Great Jones: "If [the backstroke] can be made slowly, and the downward stroke started leisurely, there may be any amount of effort without cause for worry."

When you get near the ball, rip it. Hit it hard. Have at it. What's the word? *Wallop*.

❖

GOLFFIRMATION
144

A Supreme Surrender

FEW PEOPLE give up golf. Sure, a goodly number take a break from the game, over-matched by its vexations. But the urge is hard to quell, and most prodigals return, months or years or maybe even decades later.

Legal legend Supreme Court Justice Learned Hand was one of the few who managed to stay permanently retired. His reasoning is a tribute to your persistence. This man of tremendous achievement stowed his sticks permanently because he felt that his struggles with the game revealed, not a physical limitation, but the weakness of his character. Apparently, he couldn't take it.

You may not be one of the finest legal minds in history, but at least you don't flinch from the revelation that you are but a paltry thing.

❖

GOLFFIRMATION
145

All Men Are Created Equal

CLAUDE HARMON was among the best golfers who never became a tournament professional. He won the 1948 Masters by five shots and worked for years as club pro at Winged Foot in Mamaroneck, New York. His line in praise of technique is worth downloading into your brain stem: "The beauty about golf is that the ball doesn't know how big you are."

❖

GOLFFIRMATION
146

Of Cal Ripken and
Getting Close to the Pin

TOM WATSON has eight trophies from majors, including a fistful of British Opens. But his greatest achievement is this condensation: "Golf is an underhanded game."

Of the gazillion metaphors deployed to describe the feel of a golf swing, this from-down-under thought will help. Imagine that you're a shortstop, scooping up a slow roller and firing it to first. In the same move in which you go down to get the ball, you're moving smoothly upward and through to make the throw. The swing is underhanded, according to the winner of five claret jugs.

❖

GOLFFIRMATION
147

Sympathy from Your Fellows

IMAGINE, IF you will, that you're a twenty-three handicap and that you're playing a monstrous par-5, six hundred yards plus. Let's imagine further that the 12th hole at Martindale Country Club in Auburn, Maine, is a man-eater. Not only long but narrow—with the Androscoggin River on the right and woods on the left. The members cherish bogeys on this baby. Let's say that somehow you, a 23, paste a tee-ball over the sprinkler heads 245 yards out there. Then you rope a 3-iron 190 yards into position A, and somehow you, a 23, hit the sweetest 6-iron ever struck that settles eight feet left of the hole. Two paces for birdie.

Then let's say that, over the putt, you remember you're a 23, and leave it on the low side right off the blade. The ball never had a chance, and settles eighteen inches below the hole for tap-in par on one of the toughest holes in New England. But then let's say that in your disappointment, you, a 23 mind you, hurry the par putt and jerk the gimme left. Three jack from eight feet, turning birdie into bogey.

Now, for the truth about the love at the game's heart, imagine this as well. Imagine that in the instant that the par was butchered, your brother-in-law, with whom you were locked in mortal golf contest, made a sound that contained all the sorrow of the world. Imagine, if you can, being sustained in your dark moment by the half-swallowed moan of your sister's husband, the clear agony of a man who, though he benefited from your failure, understood the game too well and cared about you too much to feel anything but pain. Such is golf. Such is brotherhood.

❖

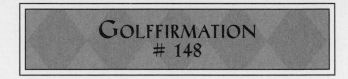

GOLFFIRMATION
148

All Quiet on the Mental Front

IT'S EASY to over-worry on the greens. The great Jones himself advised against excessive groundskeeping of the twenty feet over which your putt will roll. He felt it just as likely that some tiny pebble might knock the ball into the hole as out of it. And besides, too much care, felt Jones, puts gremlins in your head: "Bad putting is due more to the effect the green has on the player than it has upon the action of the ball."

❖

Trying Easier

So MANY of our pursuits involve trying harder. Once again, golf is contrarian; trying easier is often the key. Swing easy = ball go far. Here's a couplet, a concept, and a quip to help resist that urge to muscle up.

- Don't be a banger,
  Seek Hagen's "educated languor."
- Snead kept the expression "cool mad" in his mind to describe the effort level of his swing. You've got to hit it with authority, but stay quiet and easy, too.
- Golfer and television announcer Gary McCord's wisdom: "Conserve your energy—you have a long life ahead of you!"

❖

GOLFFIRMATION
150

Another Prohibition

THOU SHALT NOT:

. . . arrive at the tee-box of the par three that's all carry over a pond, and reach into your bag for a scrungy-looking ball. That's not exactly a Positive Mental Attitude. It's a guaranteed plunk. Take out some new ammo, and picture it rising in a graceful arc and settling hole-high and dry.

GOLFFIRMATION
151

Kill the Serpents on the Greensward

YOU'RE HUNKERED down behind your ball, peering toward the hole, trying to read your putt. It's a ball outside right, firmed. No, wait, you look again. Now, it's a straight putt. And then, as a shadow shifts across the green, suddenly the putt clearly breaks hard to the right. John Updike found just the right phrase to describe this sickening uncertainty. "The line of the putt wriggles," he wrote, "and slips around like a snake on glass."

Lord, help me to cast out the serpents, to trust my first glance. To look, assess, take my stance, and just smoothly sweep the ball.

❖

GOLFFIRMATION
152

Cherchez La Hole

JACKIE BURKE JR. beat Ken Venturi by a stroke in the 1956 Masters, coming from eight strokes behind him to do it. A few months later, Burke won the PGA championship, too. He also cut through a lot of putting confusion with this quick wisdom: "Bad putting stems from thinking how instead of where."

❖

GOLFFIRMATION
153

The Swing of Things

DON'T HIT the ball, *swing* the club, goes the refrain of countless golf instructors. If the ball gets in the way of a smooth rhythmic swing, often enough, the wisdom claims, you'll get your share of pars. Of course, asking a man with a club in his hand to *not hit* something is like telling a hungry lion *not* to pounce. The instruction blithely ignores our every forceful instinct. What do you mean don't *hit* the ball? You better believe I'm going to hit it. In fact, I'm going to clobber it!

Therein lies the durable puzzle and gift at the heart of golf. It rewards our instinct for ease, not our instinct for anger. It celebrates the fluid and easeful cadence of our hearts.

❖

The Beatific Byron

IN THE decades since Byron Nelson's eleven consecutive victories in 1945, nobody has come close to matching his string. The grouches who point out that some of his best competition was away in the armed forces fighting World War II don't understand the capriciousness of the game. Winning eleven in a row is amazing no matter the rivals.

But Lord Byron is as celebrated for his courtliness and grace as he is for his golf swing. Everybody who ever met him has some story of his gentility. So, the legend may just be true, that whenever he played a local course in an exhibition, he would always ask what the course record was; not so he could beat it, but so he could be careful not to. He figured having that plaque in the locker room meant more to a member than it would to a world famous pro.

❖

GOLFFIRMATION
155

Getting Up to Speed

MAYBE, JUST maybe, an automotive metaphor will somehow worm its way from your brain into your golf consciousness, and help you start the downswing with ease. Here goes, this one courtesy of Mickey Wright, who won 82 times on the LPGA tour, including an astonishing 50 victories over 5 years:

> You can't take a car from a dead stop and put it immediately up to 70 miles per hour. No matter how powerful your engine, you must have a gradual acceleration of speed. So it is in a golf swing.

❖

I Am All I Need to Be

WE ALL know extremely confident golfers who regularly shoot triple digits. Self-assurance is, to be sure, not enough to make you good at the game. But boy, is it necessary? "There is no other sphere," wrote P. G. Wodehouse, "in which belief in oneself has such immediate effects as it has in golf."

The goal is to somehow achieve a brilliant balance—be humbly confident, to walk up the fairways fully aware of your frailties, but nonetheless inspired by your skills. You need a kind of buoyancy, call it faith, that the smoothness and technique that dwells within will show itself in this 6-iron floated to the green. We are all flawed to be sure, but so are we all capable . . . Now, that's a golf shot.

❖

GOLFFIRMATION
157

In Search of the Sunday Entrance

THERE ARE fabulous putters who ram the ball into the hole—witness Watson and Woods—and great blade men who like to die it into the cup—Nicklaus and Crenshaw come to mind. Those who prefer the softer approach can cling to the wisdom of Stewart Maiden, the club pro at East Lake Club in Georgia, most celebrated for influencing the boy Bobby Jones.

"When the ball dies at the hole there are four doors; the ball can go in the front, or the back, or at either side. But a ball that comes up to the hole with speed on it must hit the front door in the middle; there are no side doors, and no Sunday entrance."

❖

Of Davis and His Dad

THE 1990s saw the emergence of a denigrating title held by one professional player at a time, The Best Player Never to Have Won a Major. For a few years in the mid nineties, Davis Love III was the unfortunate holder of the crown. Though he'd won his share of tournaments, he hadn't generally been at his best in the big ones. In 1996, he bogeyed 17 and 18, to play his way right out of a playoff for the U. S. Open at Oakland Hills. The demeaning title was getting heavy.

Love is the son of Davis Love Jr., who is often ranked among the great golf teachers. The father taught his boy the game, and for Love the Younger, the flavors of the game were almost inseparable from his childhood memories and love for his father, who was killed in a plane crash in 1988.

When the son got to the back nine of the 1997 PGA Championship at Winged Foot, he had the lead, and a heavy rain began. Only after he hit his approach shot on 18 hard by the flag, was it clear he'd win. As he walked up the fairway with his playing partner and closest pursuer, Justin Leonard, the rain stopped—suddenly, according to most spectators—and a huge rainbow arced overhead. Some say legend has brightened the rainbow, but at least one unromantic eyewitness swears it was the most luminous one he had ever seen. Hollywood would consider it too schmaltzy a climax, but the heavens apparently timed their glory to honor father and his son.

❖

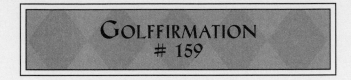

GOLFFIRMATION
159

Golf, Too, Is a Wonder of the World

THERE CAN be no question that in 1928 when Edward, the Duke of Windsor, climbed to the top of one of the Pyramids in Egypt, and teed off from the peak, he was disrespectful to antiquity. But perhaps he can be forgiven. Golf does strange things to otherwise pious men. Often, we come to see everything through a golf lens. We are obsessive seekers, pilgrims in search of what—we're not exactly sure. But golf is always there. Surely, the pyramids have never inspired the bowler or the player of bridge.

❖

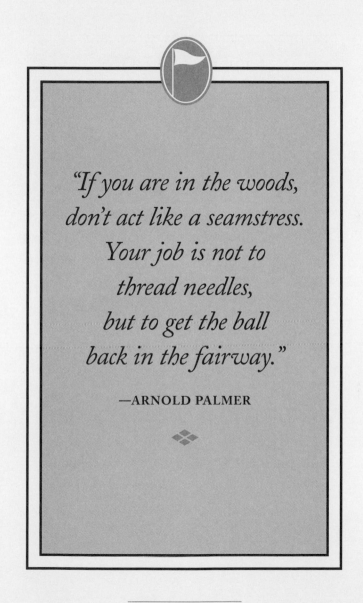

"If you are in the woods,
don't act like a seamstress.
Your job is not to
thread needles,
but to get the ball
back in the fairway."

—ARNOLD PALMER

Lightness of the Heart

GOLF IS a mere breeze as evening falls. Golf is sunlight pouring through a stand of trees. Golf is grass and hope and earth and hope and sky and hope and the way your brother hunches over a putt and hope, just one more time.

Something there is in the game that calls us on, that says continue, in spite of dubs and foozles. Golf is keep going, try again. Golf somehow lifts up the heart. Golf is tomorrow.

❖

GOLFFIRMATION
161

Come and Join the Dance

CONSIDER THE care with which golfers on the green step around and over their companions' lines to the hole. It is, of course, most often a pointless deference. For 95 out of 100 golfers, it's just as likely that a spike mark or footprint will deflect the ball into the hole, rather than away from it. Millions of times every day, golfers hop daintily, oh-so-carefully around the cup, just so the other guy can have a pristine path on which to blast a twenty-footer eighteen feet by, or miss a six-footer a good foot to the right. We credit our opponents with a surgeon's finesse; they have a sledgehammer touch. It's a delightful pretense—mannered, excessive, deliberate, and, here's the kicker, considerate of others. Imagine that, a gesture that says I believe in your skill despite everything I've seen.

Let us aspire to even more elaborate heights to high-stepping salutes, to bringing the agility of an Irish jigger to our silly stewardship of the path to the hole.

❖

GOLFFIRMATION
162

The Sweet Stroll

As YOU set out down the fairway, you can see your ball glistening in the distance, 275 yards thataway, a white fleck floating on an ocean of green. You've hit the perfect drive. With a power and grace worthy of Woods, you've smoothed the ball into position A—dead center, just an 8-iron in. And you somehow know, as you stride toward your approach shot, that you've even contrived to get a perfect lie. Surely, the ball is sitting up, just begging to be hit close; it's an egg, rich with possibilities.

Suddenly, as you walk, you notice everything. You enjoy the softness of the turf beneath your spikes, the rattle of your clubs in your bag, the breeze, the sun-glare, the perfume of the grass. As you walk, you actually notice, and appreciate, the mechanical genius of your gait. You're hot-wired by hope, attuned, by the promising position of that ball, to what E. B. White called the glory of everything.

Surely, great things might happen. The idea of

birdie even crosses your mind. Clearly, the man who hit that drive is capable of one feathered short iron hard by the hole. And, as you move, with purpose and plans toward your ball, you imagine as well that maybe things will work out at your job, and maybe you'll learn to be a better husband, father, and friend. There's ginger in your step as you dream that maybe, just maybe, the Cubs will win the World Series. Yes, the next shot may well return you to earth. But during the stroll to a truly struck shot the air itself tastes sweeter. God bless golf.

❖

Keeping Faith Through the Flood

THE NAME of the par-3 12th hole at Augusta National sounds gentle—Golden Bell. But over the years, plenty of the world's best players have come to grief on this 155-yard assassin. Any golfer who has ever lost ammo in a greenside lake will take some consolation from what happened to Tom Weiskopf during the 1980 Masters.

Weiskopf's tee-ball hit the green but then rolled, slowly, ever so slowly, back into Rae's Creek fronting the green. He went over to the drop area ahead of the tee, and proceeded to hit a sand wedge onto the green. But it too wouldn't hold, and spun back into the drink. Without saying a word, Weiskopf then proceeded to hit three more balls into the water. So he was lying 10 and still didn't have a ball in play. His sixth tee-ball finally stuck on the green, and he took two putts for a 13. Oh, by the way, the next day, in Round 2, Weiskopf drowned two more balls on the same hole before carding a 7. So, if you ever go 14 over par on consecutive assaults on a hole, just remember that, in golf, such things can happen, even to a man who won the British Open.

❖

GOLFFIRMATION
164

Ready . . . Fire . . . Aim

LEE TREVINO eventually won the British Open three times. It might have been four but for a bonehead blunder on Sunday at St. Andrew's in 1970. Trevino started the last round two strokes clear of Doug Sanders, Jack Nicklaus, and Tony Jacklin. But Nicklaus blew by him pretty quickly. And that's when Trevino really faltered.

Many of the greens at the Old Course at St. Andrew's are huge double greens, meaning one side of the green has a hole on the outward nine, and the other side has a hole for the back side. They indicate which is which by flags of different colors. On the par-5 5th, Trevino spanked an 8-iron dead on—the wrong flag! It took him three to get down, and he never recovered from the bogey.

Sure you've done some dumb things on the golf course, but you've never done anything as dumb as this Titan of the game.

The Blessing of Being Bad

ONE OF our forgivable flaws is that we tend to enjoy things at which we're skilled. Golf, to its glory, is an exception to this human inclination. Indeed, in some delightful inversion, many of the world's worst golfers seem to enjoy it the most. Why? Because the duffer gets to travel with hope in his heart. The man who is a genuine dub sees stretching out before him vast frontiers of possible improvement. For the fellow who routinely labors over 100, even a day full of bogeys is a great triumph. And all of them luxuriate in the dozens of strokes between them and par. Surely, tomorrow he won't pop up his drive, fat his second, chunk a wedge, blast out, and three-jack for a triple. The scratch player is always an inch away from disaster; the foozler a 5-iron away from hooray. The durable pleasure of the poor player is built on hope. It's the yeast that helps his heart rise.

❖

This Most Special of Sports

IF, EVEN for a moment, you ever doubt that golf is blessed, that serendipity watches over its history, consider two of the witnesses to the most celebrated shot ever struck.

It's 1935, during the final round of the second Masters, and a few years before the tournament even officially had that name. Gene Sarazen, trailing Craig Wood by 3 strokes with but 4 holes to go, smoked his 4-wood second shot over the pond fronting the par-5 15th hole. Not content to be a potential eagle, the ball pitched forward and rolled directly into the cup for a 2, a double-eagle, an albatross. Almost seventy years later, it's still the most famous shot in golf history. And who witnessed the shot heard round the world? Bobby Jones, the game's patron saint, and Walter Hagen, the embodiment of sporting style.

❖

GOLFFIRMATION
167

A Lesson from a Lousy Touch

WHO AMONG us hasn't hammered a putt past the cup and turned away in despair as the ball went screaming by the hole? One problem: Since you couldn't bear to look, now you've got no idea of the line for the ten-foot comebacker. You've got to swallow what's bitter in the cup and learn from your blunder. Have the discipline to watch the path of the botched-up putt for par, and you may be able to bend in the next one for bogey.

❖

GOLFFIRMATION
168

Leaving No Trace

LOVERS OF Mother Earth rightly complain of golf. Surely, it uses more pesticides and herbicides and water than it ought, and it often sculpts the land in less-than-natural ways. But every real golfer is a steward of the track as well. We fix ballmarks, replace divots, rake sand traps. We are determined, like the camper who loves the woods, to leave no sign of our intrusion. Like folks dedicated to caring for the planet, we have respect for generations of golfers yet to come. And respect, for anything, is good for the heart.

❖

GOLFFIRMATION
169

Of the Sky and Blades of Grass

GOLF HAPPENS on the biggest playing field of all. It's a game of great spaces. And yet, it requires that we home in, focus at the narrow level of detail. Golf teacher Harvey Penick is credited for the simple target advice, "Take dead aim." But it's no mean feat, when you're standing on the tee, under a great endless vault of sky, to aim precisely three feet left of the shorter pine tree.

Nor is it easy, when standing over a putt, to aim not just at the hole, but at a single blade of grass on the edge over which you'll bury the ball. Golf is at once macro and micro. It invites the awed gaze, but requires well-tutored attention.

❖

The Quiet at the Core

THERE'S A school of golf instruction that is inclined toward the mystical disciplines of the East. And by the East, I don't mean Baltusrol in New Jersey or Bethpage Black on Long Island, but Asia. Some savants of the game suggest the serenities of Zen. A meditative emptiness is the secret, they say, to a smooth swing and smart strategy.

Apparently, goes this thought, the golfer must shed the identities that describe him to the common world. When you're out on the course, you're not a father, not a husband, neither a software genius nor the grandchild of immigrant Poles. You are naked on the greensward—without notions of yourself to protect you.

In the novel, *The Legend of Bagger Vance*, the ghost caddie/teacher instructs Junah, the player, on the importance of the absence. "All your 'selves' are exhausted and gone," he says. "Now hit he ball with what is left." Junah's glance was desperate. "But there is nothing left," he says. Vance nods. "Exactly."

This is either phony mystical baloney or extremely important.

❖

GOLFFIRMATION
171

Will the Real You Please Stand Up?

YOUR DRIVE is just plain lovely—all of 275 yards; it rolls to a proud stop in the dead middle of the fairway. But then some guy who looks just like you hits a fatted 8-iron that travels all of thirty yards. Your third is a beauty of a wedge, soft and high, that plops and stops fifteen feet right of the hole. The 4th, a putt for par, is hit by that impostor again, and stubbed oh . . . say, about halfway to the hole. The 5th, for bogey, is tapped just right, firmly, smartly, bang, into the jar.

One minute, the game makes you feel like a king. In the next, you're the court jester. It's tempting to be annoyed by the changing roles. But that way, madness lies. Try to remember, you are both golfers—richly skilled and deeply incompetent. You have many multitudes. Don't embrace the virtuous guy and deny the feeble one. Accept both, and keep striving to improve.

❖

GOLFFIRMATION
172

The Great Eraser

GOLF CAN help you forget your troubles. It's so engrossing that for a few hours you put that registered letter from the IRS out of your mind. Somehow the challenge of trying to flop one onto the deck over a cavernous bunker momentarily erases that phrase your boss used: strategic personnel redeployment. The agonies and ecstasies of the game put to rout trivial matters like mortgage payments, medical problems, and arrest warrants. The game is relaxing because it softly commands all your mental energy, and leaves none left over for dread.

❖

GOLFFIRMATION
173

Take a Nap, Like Fred

FRED COUPLES is famous for two things: First, his final-round tee-ball on the celebrated 12th hole at Augusta, which somehow stopped rolling halfway down a steep, shaved bank above the pond. Couples hustled up to where the ball was hanging, got up and down for par, and went on to win the green jacket in 1992. The other source of Couples' fame is the languid beauty of his swing. It appears to be effortless, but in his prime, Couples could hit the ball a tremendous distance.

At the top of his swing, Couples seemed to actually stop, as though he were taking a quick nap, so he'd be sure to have enough energy for his downswing. Of course, he didn't stop up top, but boy, Couples took his time in starting his downswing, saving his energy for the moment of impact and follow-through. Get like Fred. Imagine that you're actually taking a little rest at the top of the swing. You'll find tempo and power.

❖

GOLFFIRMATION
174

The Coming of the Spring

FOR GOLFERS who live in regions with a short golf season, the winter would be unbearable but for the fact that, somehow, while hibernating, we see our swing flaws clearly. In January, while shoveling snow from your driveway in Saginaw or Bangor, you realize—eureka!—that you've been fanning the face open way too quickly. Or no, no, that's not it: Your left wrist is collapsing on your finish. Or maybe you've just got to move the ball back half an inch. Somehow, as winter wanes, the good, or better, golfer within us starts clawing his way to the surface.

Then, as the air warms and the days start to stretch, you can feel hope rising in your heart. You're a boy again—ready, yes ready, to go again.

❖

Hogan and the Highway

BEN HOGAN was no warm and cuddly fellow. He was a perfectionist, so gifted at concentration and devoted to competition that he barely spoke while on the course. Sam Snead claims the only two words Hogan ever said to him during a round were, "You're away." Surely, the Hawk would take no pleasure in being mentioned in a book as cheerfully sentimental as this one. But in addition to his achievements with the sticks, Hogan left us with a shining example of grit that requires commendation.

In the winter of 1949, Ben Hogan was at the top of the golf world. The previous year he had won the U.S. Open, the Western Open, the Vardon Trophy, the Player of the Year Award, and the money title. Then, a hammer blow hit him from the blind side. Hogan and his wife, Valerie, were driving in a fog outside Pecos, Texas, when they crashed into an oncoming Greyhound bus. Both were injured, Ben quite seriously. For a time it looked as though Hogan might not survive. His leg and hip were crushed. Few thought he'd ever play golf again. Nobody believed he'd play at the competitive level he'd set in 1948. Nobody but Hogan.

He had a stirring single-mindedness about getting back to golf. He exercised five hours a day and slowly built himself back up. Just one year after the accident, he entered the White Sulphur Springs Tournament at the Greenbrier in West Virginia. He won. Later that year, he won the U.S. Open at Merion, too, walking 36 holes on the final day on a leg and hip that had been pulverized in the accident. Golf is not for the faint of heart. Not Hogan golf, anyway.

❖

GOLFFIRMATION
176

Not How, but How Many

THE 2001 PGA Championship at Atlanta Country Club came down to the 18th hole, a monstrous 490-yard par-4 over water. David Toms had a one-shot lead over Phil Mickelson. For his second shot, Toms had just over two hundred yards to the hole, a distance that is usually no sweat for golfers of his caliber. Though the ball appeared to spectators to be sitting nicely in some light rough, it was actually down a bit and on a slightly downhill lie.

Toms assessed the situation, and decided to lay up short of the water. Though he was pretty sure that Mickelson, ahead of him in the middle of the fairway, would be on in two, he reasoned that his best shot at par was to wedge it close and drop a putt for the championship. He resisted the macho call to go for it. At the moment he pulled out the lay-up club and punched the ball down short of the lake, golf viewers across America were shouting at television screens, indicting his manhood. If his strategy failed, surely he would have been known forever as the guy who didn't bother to win the PGA Championship.

Mickelson put his second shot thirty feet from the hole. If he sank the putt, and if Toms couldn't get up and down from ninety yards, Mickelson would win with a two-shot swing on the final hole. But with remarkable calm, Toms trued a wedge and stopped it just left of the flag—twelve feet left for his first major title. If he missed, Mickelson could have two-putted for a tie. When Mickelson's birdie try stopped six inches short of the hole, Toms had one putt for victory. *Bang*—into the middle of the jar. One great decision, followed by two perfect shots, proves the point: How doesn't matter, only how many.

❖

The How of Hardpan

FORTUNE HAS smiled on you and somehow, though you hit the ball into the parking lot, you've got a clear shot to the green. The challenge: You're on some hardpan. Stay calm. Get thoughtful. Most likely, the contact with the hard ground will make the club face rotate open. To minimize that effect, grip the club nice and firmly. To allow for the clubface opening, aim for the ball to slice just a touch.

Remember, small adjustments make magic.

❖

War Is Over, Golf Begins

GOLF IS a teacher in that it makes you figure out each shot, deal with the realities of branches or bad lies. Or worse. After London got devastated by the German air force during World War II, the folks in charge at a course called Sunningdale decided to deal with the damage by turning bomb craters into bunkers.

❖

GOLFFIRMATION
179

You Will Not Be TENSE!!!

ANYBODY WHO has sought counsel about his game has been told to get the tension out of his swing. When our muscles get tense, we can't get the fluidity that generates control and power. Of course, nothing makes you stiffer than being told to relax. So try this if you feel tense standing over an approach shot to a tight pin. Lighten your grip, and when you address the ball, don't ground the club behind it. Instead, hold it just a smidge above the ground. An easier grip and the airiness of hovering the club, just a little, may let your arms soften up just a bit.

Softness is a secret to lower scores.

❖

There's Crying in Golf

SOME SAY the greatest single day in the history of golf was in 1986, when Jack Nicklaus won the Masters at age forty-six. He did it with some heroic play on the back nine—and with his son caddying for him. About the Golden Bear's tee-ball on the par-3 16th that nearly went in the hole, writer Tom Boswell remarked that if that shot *had* gone in, they could have stopped playing golf forever. Hollywood would have found the script too schmaltzy. Nicklaus said he had trouble finishing the round because his eyes kept filling with tears.

❖

GOLFFIRMATION
181

The Wisdom of the Wedge

BY NOW, everybody knows that professional golfers often aim for bunkers—especially on long par-5s. Most of us, in contrast, dread getting beached. That's because we just can't bring ourselves to trust two things every golf expert on the planet has told us: (1) The secret to getting out of the sand is to *not* hit the ball, and (2) we've got to take a big swing to hit the ball just a short way. This counter-intuitive assignment bollixes up our brains. Moreover, we get confused about precisely how far behind the ball to hit.

The truth is, precision doesn't matter. Don't focus on whether to hit two inches behind the ball or four inches behind it. Given the differences in the texture of the sand, the quality of the lie, it's impossible to make such fine-tuned calculations. Just think ballpark—somewhere between two inches and five inches behind the ball. Make a nice big swing. Bring your arms all the way back to ten o'clock. It's okay.

Trust it. The sand is going to slow the club down. Jim Flick, who lots of folks think is the best golf teacher there is, says that if you take a short swing, halfway through your mind tells your body you've got to hit the ball harder. That makes you tighten your grip, and suddenly your playing partners are dodging a skulled missile.

For now, until you're a better player, don't struggle to get the ball close. Just hit it out onto the deck. Now and then, it will nestle down hard by the hole. And now and then, even when it doesn't, you'll sink a fifteen-footer for par.

❖

"Never hurry.
Never worry,
and always remember
to smell the flowers
along the way."

—WALTER HAGEN

GOLFFIRMATION
182

Trust in Fortune

LEGENDARY BASKETBALL coach Jim Valvano, whose North Carolina State team upset a prohibitive favorite from Houston in the 1983 NCAA championship, had a strategic slogan for a team that's overmatched. "Hang around," he said, "and let yourself get lucky." His Wolfpack did just that when a desperation air-ball at the buzzer turned into an inadvertent alley-oop and a game-winning dunk. Golfers of all abilities must remember the lesson.

"Anything can happen," Bobby Jones said in his understated, straightforward way. "One must keep on hitting the ball, so that he may have a chance to enjoy a lucky break."

❖

A Knight to Remember

YOU'VE ARRIVED at the ball, taken your bag off your back and placed it in the fairway. Those plastic tripod legs have popped forward, propping the club upright, they stand at the ready– all fourteen of them—a quiverful of options, weapons awaiting your will. As you draw the 6-iron from the bag, imagine that it's a sword and you are a knight, going forth on behalf of truth, beauty, and justice. Golfers have chivalrous souls.

❖

GOLFFIRMATION
184

Trust the Stillness

THERE IS no instant more destructive to more golf swings than the eye-blink at the top of the swing. Every day, millions of us get to the transition moment—the shift from backswing to downswing—and for some reason, panic and start hurrying downward. Nobody knows exactly why, but we behave as though we have to hit the ball quickly. Apparently we don't trust the ball to stay put. The result is a lurching downward, and power lost at the top of the downswing that should be saved for the follow-through.

The question for those of us still north of 90 is how to trust the stillness of the ball and not lurch down to it. Try this, think of the ball as a devoted friend, somebody who'll always wait for you to catch up, who will always be around the next bend in the road. The ball is patient. Trust that it will always be there for you.

❖

The Blessing of a Beaten Man

EVERY GOLFER knows the moment of frustration. You've hacked your ball from the woods to the rough, then from bunker to bunker, and then, finally, onto the deck. You're lying 5, still thirty feet from the hole. Filled with self-loathing, you climb out of the bunker onto the green, heroically resist the urge to hurl your sand wedge into the pond, eyeball the putt quickly, and give it a careless whack. Tracking . . . tracking . . . tracking . . . *plock!* Middle of the jar for double bogey.

The twenty-five footer for double-bogey is so common it's even earned a vulgar golf nickname. It's a terrible feeling. You've just used the one long putt God will grant you during this round to lose the hole to your buddy's bogey.

Chances are that if the same putt were for birdie, you would have left it six feet short or nuked it into the pond. Most of us make a far higher percentage of long putts for double than we do for birdie. Why?

Because when we're putting for birdie, our anxiety about results suffocates our skill. Once the only thing at stake is whether we get a double, triple, or a snow-man, our natural ability to judge line and pace emerges from under our dread. So next time you're standing over a long one for birdie, try not caring.

❖

On Fidelity and Foursomes

"LIKE THE golf course itself, golf camaraderie is an artifice, carved from the vastness of nature; it only asks five or six hours a week, from the jocular greetings in the noontime parking lot and the parallel donning of cleats in the locker room to the shouted farewells in the dusk, as the flagsticks cast their long shadows. Within this finity, irritations, jealousies, and even spats do occur, but they are mercifully dulled and dampened by the necessary distances of the game, the traditional reticence and mannerliness of sportsmen, and the thought that it will all be over soon. As in marriage, there is sharing: we search for one another's lost balls, we comment helpfully upon one another's defective swings, we march more or less in the same direction, and we come together, like couples at breakfast and dinner, on the tees and on the greens. . . . We are, my beloved comrades and I, that afternoon's entertainment: our camaraderie has the subtle frenzy of show business, the makeup and glitter of it, as our fortunes ebb and flow and we live up to our roles or momentarily step out of them. The good feelings that golf breeds are inseparable from its aura of being out in the open— of being enacted within a wide and breezy transparency that leaves no shortcoming hidden and no happy stroke uncongratulated."

—*John Updike*

❖

Haiku for Hills

THE JAPANESE love two things: golf and *haiku*, the ancient art of a seventeen-syllable poem. When your ball's not on the level, remember this blend of Japanese joys:

> When faced with
> Ground sloping up or down,
> Move the ball toward your
> Higher foot.

❖

GOLFFIRMATION
188

Of Golf and Poetry

IN DAYS of yore, philosophers imagined that inspiration came to the creative mind in *sweven*, a dream-state halfway between sleep and consciousness. The fully awake mind was too alert to let visions swim up from the deep. The sleepy mind was too dulled to be visionary. But in the middle . . . ah, there was artfulness. One of the strong currents of golf's mental game is the ambition to achieve this kind of *sweven*, to be somehow at once mindful and alert, yet uninhibited by conscious thought. It's a tough state to achieve, but you're a clever guy. Wake up and dream! If it were easy, everyone would do it.

❖

GOLFFIRMATION
189

God Grant Us Grit

 GARY PLAYER is celebrated for his determination. Something inside won't let him quit, even under the most adverse of circumstances.

The result: more than a few stirring comebacks. Once during the 36-hole semifinals of the World Match Play Championship, he came back from seven holes down after the morning 18 to beat Tony Lema. But his signature comeback was at the 1978 Masters.

Forty-two years old at the time, Player began the final round 7 shots behind Hubert Green. Early in the round, he didn't make much of a move. But he exploded over the last ten holes, birdieing seven of them, for a back nine 30 and a one-shot win. That day, he was paired with a young Seve Ballesteros, the Spaniard who would go on to win the Masters twice, and the British Open thrice. Some believe that it was bearing witness to this magnificent performance by Player that galvanized Ballesteros into the extraordinary competitor he was about to become.

Keep in mind the aptness of Gary's name. Be a player.

❖

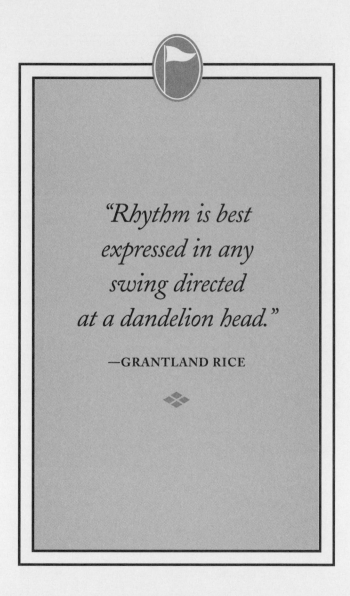

*"Rhythm is best
expressed in any
swing directed
at a dandelion head."*

—GRANTLAND RICE

GOLFFIRMATION
190

A Limerick on a Bad Lie

 THERE ONCE was a drive in a divot,
Big deal, you're a golfer, deal wiv'it,
Stay down and through,
Strike the ball true,
Bad breaks, part of life, let's live it.

❖

The Gift of Not-so-Great Expectations

THOUGH IT's debatable if Bobby Jones is the greatest golfer ever, it's clear that he's the best combination of player and theorist. His book, *Bobby Jones on Golf*, is a remarkable instructional volume, full of practical tips and enlivening excursions into the nature of the swing and the game. This passage from the golf classic describes a key difference between a powerful effort and effortless power:

We would all do better could we only realize that the length of a drive depends not upon the brute force applied but upon the speed of the club head. It is a matter of velocity rather than of physical effort of the kind that bends crowbars and lifts heavy weights. I like to think of a golf club as a weight attached to my hands by an imponderable medium, to which a string is a close approximation, and I like to feel that I am throwing it at the ball with much the same motion I should use in cracking a whip. By the simile, I mean to convey the idea of a supple and lightning-quick action of the wrists in striking—a sort of flailing action.

GOLFFIRMATION
192

Of Final Holes and Last Legs

WE DON'T generally think of golf as a game that requires physical courage. But the story of Ken Venturi at the 1964 U.S. Open is an exception. Venturi had some early success on the tour, but then in 1962 he developed a pinched nerve in his neck. The condition got worse and worse until one side of his body was close to paralyzed. He couldn't play at all. But over the course of a couple of years, he fought his way back and qualified for the U.S. Open to be held at Congressional Country Club, outside Washington, D.C.

Back then, the last day of the tournament included 36 holes. The temperature in D.C. was in the nineties—complete with the capital's trademark humidity. After the first 18 holes, Venturi's health seemed so poor that USGA officials asked a doctor to walk with him during the afternoon round. Though at several points, it seemed as though he might pass out, Venturi played well and somehow had the lead coming to 18. Walking up the fairway, he stumbled twice and almost fell. He looked more like a punch-drunk boxer than a golfer, and it seemed as though he might not be able to finish the round. But he somehow did, closing out with a par, before collapsing back in the clubhouse, trophy secured.

When you're trudging up the 18th fairway, perfectly healthy but dog-tired, remember Venturi's march and step lively.

❖

GOLFFIRMATION
193

A Limerick Fix

 THERE ONCE was a golfer who topped.
He leaned back on his heels, couldn't stop.
When he bent more his knees
And his waist, he was pleased,
With the weight shift, his score it did drop.

GOLFFIRMATION
194

When Bad Things Happen,
Comebacks Get Possible

YOUR BALL is sitting wedged between two boulders. Or maybe it's under three inches of water. Or trapped under a root. Or buried, but for two dimples, in the deepest bunker in North America. Hey! That's not bad news. It's an opportunity, a chance to strike a historic blow, a shot that people will remember forever, about which your playing partners will tell their kids. Don't be demoralized by the ball gone wrong. Anybody can smile in the sunshine. We're judged by how we do when things look bleak. And the next time your drive goes screaming into the forest primeval, be of stout heart. That just might be the beginning of a legendary par.

❖

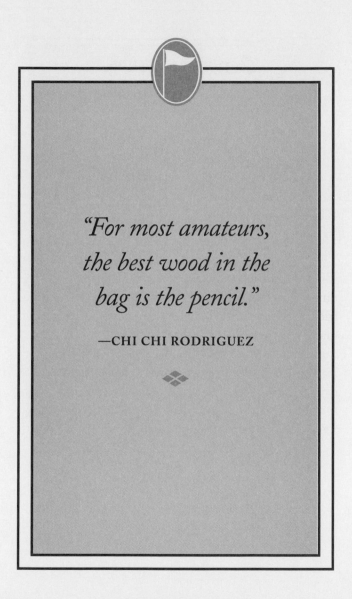

"*For most amateurs,
the best wood in the
bag is the pencil.*"

—CHI CHI RODRIGUEZ

GOLFFIRMATION
195

Pride Goeth Before High Scores

WE OFTEN take a silly pride in being able to hit each of our clubs a long way. Who cares if you need an 8-iron or a 7-iron to cover 150 yards. This preoccupation with distance just causes nine out of ten approach shots to come up short. The trick is to *get there*. Which implement you use couldn't matter less.

Henry Beard had a good line that captures the catastrophe that awaits the golfer who hasn't learned this crucial lesson: "When your shot has to carry over a water hazard, you can either hit one more club or two more balls."

❖

The Close of Day

CHERISH THE beauty of a golf course at dusk. The cool has come. The light, now orange, slants through long shadows. The birds come alive again, deer or rabbits enlivened by the sun's fade venture into a fairway. A peaceable kingdom is born. The players, weary and yet ennobled by staying the course, putt out to rising of the merest wind, the hush that comes with good night.

❖

GOLFFIRMATION
197

Till the Tee-Time Tomorrow

As ALWAYS, the last word belongs to Shivas Irons, the very spirit of golf, created for all of us by Michael Murphy in the landmark *Golf in the Kingdom*. The plain truth that explains the addiction:

> Golf is for smellin' heather and cut grass and walkin' fast across the countryside and feelin' the wind and watchin' the sun go down and seein' your friends hit good shots and hittin' some yerself. It's love and it's feeling the splendor o' this good world.

❖